Vulnerability and Long-term Care in Europe

Agar Brugiavini • Ludovico Carrino
Cristina Elisa Orso • Giacomo Pasini

Vulnerability and Long-term Care in Europe

An Economic Perspective

palgrave
macmillan

Agar Brugiavini
Department of Economics
Ca' Foscari University
Venice, Italy

Ludovico Carrino
Department of Global Health & Social Medicine
King's College
London, United Kingdom

Cristina Elisa Orso
Department of Economics
Ca' Foscari University
Venice, Italy

Giacomo Pasini
Department of Economics
Ca' Foscari University
Venice, Italy

ISBN 978-3-319-68968-5 ISBN 978-3-319-68969-2 (eBook)
https://doi.org/10.1007/978-3-319-68969-2

Library of Congress Control Number: 2017955675

Cover illustration: Pattern adapted from an Indian cotton print produced in the 19th century

Printed on acid-free paper

This Palgrave Pivot imprint is published by Springer Nature
The registered company is Springer International Publishing AG
The registered company address is: Gewerbestrasse 11, 6330 Cham, Switzerland

Preface

This book provides a novel approach to investigating the effects of longevity on the welfare of Europeans, focusing the attention on the need and the provision of insurance in the form of long-term care. The motivation behind this study is the extraordinary improvement in life expectancy experienced in the last century in Europe and the implied changes in the demographic structure of society, coupled with a significant exposure to vulnerability experienced at older ages. Important differences in health conditions emerge in Europe for different socio-economic groups, which will translate in a marked inequality of well-being at older ages. The book fills a gap in the literature by pointing to the economic relevance of long-term care in view of increasing rates of care-dependent older people at a time when welfare systems are retrenching. The book presents an overview of the basic concepts of vulnerability and dependency: older people who are *dependent* on others' help with their basic activities of daily living, and are unable to maintain an *acceptable* level of well-being. We enhance the policy relevance of long-term care insurance by providing a detailed taxonomy of the forms of coverage existing in Europe and looking at the range of services required by individuals with a reduced degree of functional capacity, physical or cognitive. We are the first to make use of detailed micro-data at the individual on large surveys representative of the European population age 50 and over, such as the English Longitudinal Study on Ageing (ELSA) and the Survey of Health, Ageing and Retirement in Europe (SHARE) in order to support our investigation with sound empirical evidence. We document, by making use of individual data, the efficacy of the different long-term are provisions in different institutional contexts and simulate "counterfactual" regimes.

We argue that there is scope for harmonization both on terms of assessment-of-needs procedures and in terms of long-term care provisions. The assessment procedures of each country or region are largely affected by a sluggish and often complex legislation, with little attention being paid to the fast-changing health conditions of older people, to the extent that many countries ignore cognitive impairments in their protocols while cognitive decline is becoming a major source of dependency. Long-term care insurance is extremely fragmented and a significant variability of benefits and provisions emerges even at a local level. We identify the most effective methodologies to provide a robust assessment of needs as well as the efficacy of the different policies in providing good care and ultimately guaranteeing well-being to older people.

This book is an ideal compendium for academics and public health operators who want to learn about vulnerability in old age and its implications and for policy makers who face decisions in the domains of dependency and long-term care.

Acknowledgements

This study uses data from SHARE Waves 1, 2, 3 (SHARELIFE), 4, 5 and 6 (DOIs: 10.6103/SHARE.w1.600, 10.6103/SHARE.w2.600, 10.6103/SHARE.w3.600, 10.6103/SHARE.w4.600, 10.6103/SHARE.w5.600, 10.6103/SHARE.w6.600), see Börsch-Supan et al. (2013) for methodological details. The SHARE data collection has been primarily funded by the European Commission through FP5 (QLK6-CT-2001-00360), FP6 (SHARE-I3: RII-CT-2006-062193, COMPARE: CIT5-CT-2005-028857, SHARELIFE: CIT4-CT-2006-028812) and FP7 (SHARE-PREP: N°211909, SHARE-LEAP: N°227822, SHARE M4: N°261982). Additional funding from the German Ministry of Education and Research, the Max Planck Society for the Advancement of Science, the US National Institute on Aging (U01_AG09740-13S2, P01_AG005842, P01_AG08291, P30_AG12815, R21_AG025169, Y1-AG-4553-01, IAG_BSR06-11, OGHA_04-064, HHSN271201300071C) and from various national funding sources is gratefully acknowledged (see www.share-project.org).

This study also uses data from ELSA Wave 7. ELSA data were made available through the UK Data Archive. ELSA was developed by a team of researchers based at the NatCen Social Research, University College London and the Institute for Fiscal Studies. The data were collected by NatCen Social Research. The funding is provided by the National Institute of Aging in the United States, and a consortium of UK government departments co-ordinated by the Office for National Statistics. The developers and funders of ELSA and the archive bear no responsibility for the analyses or interpretations presented here.

The authors wish to thank Mauricio Avendaño, Vincenzo Atella, Cinzia Di Novi, Silvio Giove, Stefania Maggi and Alberto Pilotto, as well as participants to the ILPN Long-Term Care Policy Network (London, 2014 and 2016) and the VIU Summer Institute of Ageing (Venice, 2017) for their valuable comments on previous versions of this book. Ludovico Carrino acknowledges the financial support of Fondazione Farmafactoring (Research Award 2015) and of the Economic and Social Research Council (award ES/P000487/1).

Contents

About the Authors

Agar Brugiavini is Professor of Economics at Ca' Foscari University of Venice, she is Director of the Ca' Foscari International College and Research Affiliate of the Institute for Fiscal Studies-IFS, London. She has been co-Editor of *Research in Economics* and has contributed to many volumes of the NBER project "Social Security around the World".

Ludovico Carrino is Research Associate at the Department of Global Health & Social Medicine at King's College London and affiliated to the Department of Economics of the Ca' Foscari University of Venice. He is Adjunct Professor at the University of Trieste. His research interests are in the areas of Applied Ageing, Health and Welfare Economics.

Cristina Elisa Orso is Post-Doctoral Researcher and Adjunct Professor at Ca' Foscari University of Venice. Her research interests include Health and Ageing Economics, Development and Gender Economics.

Giacomo Pasini is Associate Professor at Ca' Foscari University of Venice. He is also a Research Fellow of Netspar, the international network for Studies on Pension, Ageing and Retirement. Professor Pasini recently published in field journals such as *Health Economics*, the *Review of Financial Studies* and the *Review of Finance*.

List of Abbreviations and Acronyms

ADL	Activities of Daily Living
ELSA	English Longitudinal Study of Ageing
EU	European Union
iADL	instrumental Activities of Daily Living
LTC	long-term care
OECD	Organisation for Economic Co-operation and Development
SHARE	Survey on Health, Ageing and Retirement in Europe
WHO	World Health Organisation

List of Figures

List of Tables

CHAPTER 1

Introduction

Abstract This chapter introduces the topics covered in this book. The effective coverage and the overall quality in terms of the well-being of the target population reached by a given long-term care (LTC) programme are the result of a complex interaction of a number of determinants, which require a careful analysis of the different steps involved in the process. Hence, presenting a complete picture, analysing a detailed taxonomy and drawing some useful conclusions about the risk of vulnerability and the extent of dependency in old age represents a challenge because of the variety of solutions adopted in Europe. Our analysis makes two substantial contributions: the estimation of the coverage rates results from country-specific definitions of vulnerability, which have not been considered to date, without the imposition of any a priori criteria; second, the use of micro-data allows us to control for the different epidemiologic characteristics of European countries.

Keywords Ageing • Long-term care eligibility criteria • Vulnerability • Long-term care coverage • Health equity

The extraordinary improvement in life expectancy and health conditions experienced in the last century in many developed countries has changed the demographic structure of society in many significant ways. On average, people in Europe live longer and enjoy better health; however, a sig-

A. Brugiavini et al., *Vulnerability and Long-term Care in Europe*,
https://doi.org/10.1007/978-3-319-68969-2_1

nificant degree of health inequality among different socio-economic groups is also emerging (e.g., Case and Deaton, 2015). In this context, the economic relevance of formal long-term care (LTC) has been growing over recent years, and the rates of care-dependent older people in need of LTC are expected to increase in future. People are being assigned greater responsibility for their geriatric care yet the general capacity and willingness to provide for long-term care varies greatly. Very often, individuals are unprepared for the onset of limitations and the loss of autonomy in old age and do not save enough for the high and prolonged expenses necessary to cope with long-term care. The private insurance market is affected by the usual adverse selection problems, hence making public provisions for LTC essential for a large share of the population. For these reasons, several European countries have implemented social care reforms and insurance arrangements to provide new forms of community care, domiciliary care and home care insurance, alongside the more traditional policies. The aim is to provide a sustainable instrument of care that could prevent institutionalization while easing the burden on family members and enhancing the financial sustainability of public programmes (Colombo & Mercier, 2012; Costa-Font et al., 2008; Gori & Fernandez, 2015; Ranci & Pavolini, 2012; Rechel et al., 2013). However, there is an intense debate over the impact of budget reductions, resulting from the introduction of these reforms on the health and social care systems. For instance, a recent analysis, which focused on the United Kingdom, highlights a potential link between disinvestment in both health and social care and the increase of mortality rates, especially among older people (Hiam, Dorling, Harrison, & McKee, 2017a, 2017b).

Long-term care (LTC) refers to a set of policies and interventions aimed at covering the vulnerability risks that typically affect older people. More specifically, LTC is defined as a range of services required by persons with a reduced degree of functional capacity, physical or cognitive, who are *dependent* on others' help with their basic activities of daily living for an extended period of time, and are unable to maintain an *acceptable* level of well-being.[1] Older people are more likely to suffer from these conditions and limitations which reduce their autonomy in life, but it should be clear that this is not a one-to-one relationship: other groups of the population may be *vulnerable* in a general sense, while many older people lead their life free from any limitations or illnesses. This book presents an overview of the basic concepts of vulnerability and dependency along with LTC provisions and legislations in several European countries. A thorough discussion on the notion of well-being per se is beyond the scope of our analysis: we focus on the institutional set-up prevailing in Europe and document the actual level of vulnerability, measure eligibility conditions and estimate the degree of effective LTC coverage. To this end, we make use of detailed micro-data at the individual level on large surveys representative of the European population age 50 and over.

An important distinction that should be made upfront is between "formal" care and "informal" care: the former requires some form of legislation defined in a contractual relationship between the caregiver (an individual or an institution) and the beneficiary, the latter is typically provided within the household by family and friends. Furthermore, formal care can be provided by private care units or professionals or public institutions, each requiring a different degree of structure and organization. In the case of private LTC, services are usually provided by professionals (such as nurses) and are purchased at conditions defined by the market; however, both public and private LTC may entail a variety of welfare provisions (in-kind or in-cash) which will be detailed in the remainder of the book.

Hence, besides the definition and measurement of vulnerability it is relevant to refer to the issue of *utilization* of formal LTC. In economic terms, one could draw an analogy with the standard demand and supply model, whereby, in a given market, the demand curve and the supply curve meet to generate the equilibrium outcomes. Just as in the standard competitive equilibrium paradigm, the underlying mechanism is the interaction between many different agents, i.e., buyers and sellers. In fact, the utilization of LTC provisions requires some degree of interaction between the applicant and the institution providing the service (in-kind or in-cash). However, differently from a standard economic market mechanism the utilization of LTC has several steps related to the interaction of clinical conditions, on the one hand, and the nature of vulnerability risks, on the other. A commonly adopted approach describes this interaction under three perspectives: the *availability* of the service; its *accessibility*; and its *utilization* (i.e., realized accessibility) by the applicant (see Levesque, Harris, and Russell [2013] for a detailed review of this approach and its variants).

Availability pertains to the existence of any supply of LTC in the nation/region/community where the applicant lives, i.e., it concerns the "supply side" of the process. In the context of public welfare provisions, this points to the existence of system and a legal framework that regulates one or more care programmes. *Accessibility* refers to the circumstances determining whether an individual can or cannot benefit from a programme, given her health and socio-economic characteristics. In other words, differently from a competitive market approach, only a subset of individuals can enjoy the benefit, and the selection is based on a number of eligibility conditions, which are unrelated to the availability of resources or to the pricing, but rather to specific conditions of the potential beneficiary. Our discussion will show that, indeed, individuals with the same clinical profile may be eligible to access for LTC services under one legislation while being ineligible under others. *Utilization* (or *realized accessibility*) refers to the extent to which an individual can benefit from a programme, once she/he has been awarded eligibility.

Because of these features, the effective coverage and the overall quality in terms of well-being of the target population reached by a given LTC programme are the result of a complex interaction of determinants, which require a careful analysis of the different steps involved in the process. Hence, presenting a complete picture, analysing a detailed taxonomy and drawing some useful conclusions the risk of vulnerability and the extent of dependency in old age represent a challenge due to the variety of solutions adopted in Europe.

Our analysis makes two substantial contributions: the estimation of the coverage rates results from country-specific definitions of vulnerability, which have not been exploited to date, without imposing a priori criteria; second, the use of micro-data allows us to control for the different epidemiologic characteristics of European countries.

In Chap. 2, we address the substantial differences existing among the Western European LTC legislations (namely, Austria, Belgium, the Czech Republic, England, France, Germany, Italy and Spain), both between and within countries, in terms of defining the target population in need-of-LTC. Although the majority of programmes cover functional (mostly Activities of Daily Living [ADL] and Instrumental Activities of Daily Living [iADL]) and cognitive limitations, the assessment process appears in most countries as a patchwork of different rules and practices. These differences can give rise also to differential measurement criteria: the health outcomes may attract different weights within an assessment scale, with some limitations being given more importance than others in determining eligibility and there are legislations that characterize some deficit as necessary and/or sufficient for eligibility.

In Chap. 3, we detail the main LTC legislations in the selected countries. Each country profile includes up-to-date legislative information, details on the assessment of need procedures, the eligibility rules and the in-kind or in-cash benefits for the eligible population. The chapters for Belgium and Italy are organized at the regional level, given the high degree of heterogeneity of the local LTC programmes.

In Chap. 4, using micro-data from the Survey of Health Ageing and Retirement in Europe (SHARE) and the English Longitudinal Study on Ageing (ELSA), we estimate the potential coverage of each specific LTC programme, disentangling the differences between countries' coverage rates in a population and the effects of legislation. More precisely, by applying each piece of legislation on the standard population of SHARE and ELSA, we generate a set of comparable "directly-adjusted" eligibility rates (i.e., the share of the standard population that would be covered by each programme). Furthermore, we perform a pair-wise comparison of programmes' inclusiveness through a counterfactual analysis (indirect adjustment), i.e., simulating the adoption of a region's legislation on another region's population.

In the final chapter, Chap. 5, we address the "health equity" issue related to the access to formal home care services across a set of European countries. We make use of the individual-level eligibility index developed in Chap. 4, and relate it to the most relevant "covariates". The novelty of this chapter is that, by using the SHARE and the ELSA data, we can analyse the effect of adverse health shocks occurring during individuals' lives as captured by a cumulative measure of health deterioration. The purpose of the analysis is to compare individuals with similar socio-economic backgrounds and similar health histories, by distinguishing those who may face the need for LTC as a result of a health shock: this is the "demand side" of the programme. However, depending on the LTC legislation to which these individuals are exposed, they will have different probabilities of access to care and different coverage, i.e. there is also a "supply side". We describe how different LTC systems cope with the "cumulative health disadvantage".

Notes

1. This personal care component is frequently provided in combination with help with basic medical services, such as nursing care (help with wound dressing, pain management, medication, health monitoring), as well as pre-

vention, rehabilitation or services of palliative care. Long-term care services can also be combined with lower-level care related to domestic help or less demanding tasks. LTC can be provided in the recipient's own dwelling (*home-based care/domiciliary care*) rather than in nursing homes or residential care facilities (*residential/institutional care*). In this chapter, we will concentrate on the LTC programmes that offer in-kind or in-cash benefits for home-based care, the so-called *formal care* provided by professional nurses or social workers (as opposed to the *informal care* provided by the dependent's family and friends) (OECD, 2013).

References

Case, A., & Deaton, A. (2015). Rising morbidity and mortality in midlife among white non-Hispanic Americans in the 21st century. *Proceedings of the National Academy of Sciences*, *112*(49), 15078–15083. https://doi.org/10.1073/pnas.1518393112.

Colombo, F., & Mercier, J. (2012). Help wanted? Fair and sustainable financing of long-term care services. *Applied Economic Perspectives and Policy*, *34*(2), 316–332.

Costa-Font, J., Wittenberg, R., Patxot, C., Comas-Herrera, A., Gori, C., di Maio, A., … Rothgang, H. (2008). Projecting long-term care expenditure in four European Union member states: The influence of demographic scenarios. *Social Indicators Research*, *86*(2), 303–321.

Gori, C., & Fernandez, J.-L. (2015). *Long-term care reforms in OECD countries.* Bristol: Policy Press.

Hiam, L., Dorling, D., Harrison, D., & McKee, M. (2017a). What caused the spike in mortality in England and Wales in January 2015? *Journal of the Royal Society of Medicine*, *110*(4), 131–137.

Hiam, L., Dorling, D., Harrison, D., & McKee, M. (2017b). Why has mortality in England and Wales been increasing? An iterative demographic analysis. *Journal of the Royal Society of Medicine*, *110*(4), 153–162.

Levesque, J.-F., Harris, M. F., & Russell, G. (2013). Patient-centred access to health care: Conceptualising access at the interface of health systems and populations. *International Journal for Equity in Health*, *12*, 18.

OECD. (2013). *A good life in old age?* Paris: OECD Publishing.

Ranci, C., & Pavolini, E. (2012). *Reforms in long-term care policies in Europe: Investigating institutional change and social impacts.* New York: Springer.

Rechel, B., Grundy, E., Robine, J.-M., Cylus, J., Mackenbach, J. P., Knai, C., & McKee, M. (2013). Ageing in the European Union. *The Lancet*, *381*(9874), 1312–1322.

CHAPTER 2

The Concept of Vulnerability: Clinical Versus Policy Perspectives

Abstract In Chap. 2, we address the substantial differences existing among the Western European LTC legislations (namely, Austria, Belgium, the Czech Republic, England, France, Germany, Italy and Spain), both between and within countries, on defining the target population in need of long-term care (LTC). Although the majority of programmes cover functional (mostly Activities of Daily Living [ADL] and Instrumental Activities of Daily Living [iADL]) and cognitive limitations, the assessment process appears in most countries as a patchwork of different rules and practices. These differences can give rise also to differential measurement criteria: the health outcomes may attract different weights within an assessment scale; some limitations are given more importance than others in determining eligibility; and there are legislations that characterize some deficit as necessary and/or sufficient for eligibility.

Keywords Needs assessment process • Access to care • Target older population • ADL/iADL limitations • Cognitive limitations

The concept of vulnerability and the identification of the vulnerability condition has been the object of several research programmes as well as a central theme in the policy debate for several of Europe's welfare systems. The attention is often devoted to an "objective" definition as opposed to a subjective perception of vulnerability, in an effort to make the definition

A. Brugiavini et al., *Vulnerability and Long-term Care in Europe*,
https://doi.org/10.1007/978-3-319-68969-2_2

somewhat operational. However, the roots of the debate pertain to the philosophical domain: in the search for a comprehensive and exhaustive description of vulnerability a direct link to the concept of *dignity* emerges (Brock, 1989; Gallagher, Li, Wainwright, Jones, & Lee, 2008; Nordenfelt, 2004; Nussbaum & Sen, 1993). This fundamental nexus between the two concepts has shaped the ideas and the work of many academics and scientists, but also the approach of several institutions, organization and policy makers. The OECD, for example, acknowledges that "protecting the right to a life in dignity of frail older people is becoming a major policy challenge" (OECD, 2013).

This chapter offers details on the major European programmes of home-based care for the older population.

In the attempt to obtain a tractable definition of vulnerability a distinction has been drawn between the general and universal *human dignity*, i.e., a specific value of mankind, which cannot be taken away from the human being as long as s/he is alive and the so-called "*dignity of identity*" related to the integrity of the subject's body and mind (Nordenfelt, 2004). Vulnerability corresponds to a deterioration of the dignity of identity.

Although the philosophical framework described above provides the guiding principles of the shared notion of vulnerability, the basic concept remains rather opaque. A general consensus has been reached on the fact that *frailty* and vulnerability in general are undesirable conditions. In particular, the fact that vulnerability is not "directly observable" and that there is no simple diagnosis of an illness or a disease, generates a gap between the deep fundamental theory and its applied counterpart. As a result, the methods developed to measure and operationalize the theory, with the ultimate goal of preventing or delaying the occurrence of vulnerability, has produced the most compelling evidence on what we can refer to as vulnerability. The clinical literature has produced a rich and extensive body of evidence on the nature of vulnerability [see, e.g., Markle-Reid and Browne (2003)], which also emphasizes the discord between the unidimensional and the multidimensional approach. As a result, several indexes have been proposed as instruments to measure vulnerability [see, e.g., De Vries et al. (2011)]: while this body of research has brought about significant progress in understanding the mechanisms the consequences of vulnerability, a gold standard for its definition has not yet emerged.

Parallel to the issue of investigating the concept and measurement of vulnerability we intend to document the rules of the existing public LTC systems in Europe. It is useful to point out that the access to public LTC is normally implemented in two sequential steps. First, an *assessment-of-need* is performed in order to build a "vulnerability profile" of the applicant; second, a decision on their eligibility status is taken by comparing the vulnerability profile with a set of eligibility rules defined by the legislation. Thus, legislations discriminate, at the extensive margin, between eligible and non-eligible individuals (i.e., whether or not an individual should have *access* to the programme) while at the intensive margin they determine the extent to which a recipient can benefit from the programme (i.e., the degree of eligibility), which determines the level of *utilization* of the service.

In this chapter, we present an up-to-date survey on both the definition and measurement of vulnerability through the adoption of a "clinical approach", and the eligibility conditions for LTC as emerging from the assessment of needs approach.

2.1 The Clinical Approach to Vulnerability

Vulnerability relates to physiological changes that are typically observed in older people. The medical literature describes a multidimensional condition where the keywords are: *frailty*, *disability/dependency* and *comorbidity*. Fried, Ferrucci, Darer, Williamson, and Anderson (2004) provide a detailed set of characteristics which identify these conditions. The state of *frailty* is "a clinical syndrome characterised by multiple characteristics including weight loss, and/or fatigue, weakness, low activity, slow motor performance, balance and gait abnormalities", together with a potential cognitive deficit. *Disability* is defined as "difficulty or dependency in carrying out activities essential to independent living, including essential roles, tasks needed for self-care and living independently in a home, and desired activities important to one's quality of life". Finally, *comorbidity* is "the concurrent presence of two or more medically diagnosed diseases in the same individual, with the diagnosis of each contributing disease based on established and widely recognised criteria".

Being able to evaluate an individual's vulnerability status, and summarizing it in a single, encompassing measure is the only tractable way to assess the need for care, but it has to overcome several conceptual hurdles. First, *frailty*, *disability* and *comorbidity* are distinct, but overlapping concepts. Frailty and comorbidity are jointly predictors of disability, which, in turn, can exacerbate frailty and comorbidity. At the same time, comorbidity has been proved to contribute to a deterioration in terms of frailty

(Fried et al., 2004). The problem is that not all the physiological changes that underlie frailty and disability lead to a disease status, so that they are neither necessary nor sufficient conditions for ageing or death (Rockwood & Mitnitski, 2007). In particular, frailty is considered a pre-disability state and that therefore, unlike disability, it is reversible [there is "potential for intervention", in the words of Conroy (2009)]. More generally, the association between vulnerability and ageing is strong, yet not all older adults are vulnerable (De Vries et al., 2011; Pel-Littel, Schuurmans, Emmelot-Vonk, & Verhaar, 2009).

The most prevalent symptoms of vulnerability are usually identified with a loss of autonomy in the "Activities of Daily Living" (henceforth ADL), as well as in the "instrumental Activities of Daily Living" (henceforth iADL). The ADL taxonomies developed by Katz, Downs, Cash, and Grotz (1970) (the Katz index) and by Mahoney and Barthel (1965) (the Barthel index) assess how an individual performs, without assistance, in main functioning domains such as bathing, dressing, toileting, transferring, continence and feeding. The Barthel index also evaluates controlling bladder, moving from chair to bed, walking on a level surface, and ascending and descending stairs The iADL scale (Lawton & Brody, 1969) comprises eight tasks: ability to use the telephone, shopping, food preparation, housekeeping, doing laundry, mode of transportation, responsibility for their own medications and the ability to handle finances. Since the latter set of tasks requires a more complex neuropsychological organization than ADL, the iADL scale measures less severe levels of vulnerability.[1] Besides observing limitations in ADL and/or iADL, other outcomes may be relevant, including limitations in mobility, deterioration in nutritional status, cognition and endurance, weight loss, lowered serum cholesterol levels, and increasing sensitivity to change [see, e.g., Pel-Littel et al. (2009)] for a detailed analysis). Indeed, psychological and emotional state, as well as coping style and social environment, may influence disability as much as the biological or physiological factors (De Vries et al., 2011).

All these risk factors interact in multiple and complex ways, so that different combinations of deficits or different comorbidities imply different levels of vulnerability, which explains why there is no "gold standard" in the definition or, in fact, in the measurement of vulnerability (Fried et al., 2004; Fulop et al., 2010; Sourial et al., 2010; Pilotto and Ferrucci, 2011; Rodríguez-Mañas et al., 2013). Recent clinical research has produced tools which focus on the implementation of the theory, as reviewed by

Clegg, Young, Iliffe, Rikkert, and Rockwood (2013), Pel-Littel et al. (2009), De Vries et al. (2011) and Pialoux, Goyard, and Lesourd (2012). The *frailty index* in Mitnitski, Mogilner, and Rockwood (2001) and Rockwood and Mitnitski (2007) links the condition of frailty to the accumulation of deficits, while Pilotto et al. (2013) develop and validate a multidimensional index of vulnerability and mortality based on a multidimensional assessment schedule (SVaMA) adopted in several Italian regions. Finally, the World Health Organization (WHO) developed an instrument—the International Classification of Functioning (ICF)—to provide public institutions with a "consistent and internationally comparable" tool to collect data on vulnerability, adopting a bio-psychosocial perspective on the phenomenon (WHO, 2002).

2.2 Dimensions and Main Outcomes of Vulnerability in the European Landscape

In order to determine access to care, public institutions implementing LTC services need to draw a line in the continuum of vulnerability situations in which individuals may be observed. This way they can identify *when* an individual suffers from limitations which are severe enough to the extent that she can be granted an LTC benefit. As we argued, the absence of a standardized clinical definition of vulnerability is likely to be reflected into substantial differences in need assessment and eligibility rules between programmes, and the recent literature has indeed highlighted the striking heterogeneity existing across Europe when it comes to social care and long-term care. The work by Colombo and Mercier (2012), as well as reports by the European Commission (2015), and works by Gori and Fernandez (2015), Eleftheriades and Wittenberg (2013), Da Roit and Le Bihan (2010) and Comas-Herrera et al. (2003), detailed how different LTC schemes and different definitions of vulnerability may be the outcome of heterogeneous policy objectives, philosophies and institutional frameworks. Lack of harmonization in the operationalized definition of vulnerability, which can take place even within a single country, has been discussed by Jiménez-Martín and Prieto (2010) for Spain and Bakx, Meijer, Schut, and Doorslaer (2014) for the Netherlands, while Eleftheriades and Wittenberg (2013) and Comas-Herrera et al. (2003) provided an overview for several countries.

This chapter provides a taxonomy for the main LTC programmes existing in Western Europe, focussing the attention on eligibility for LTC and on the definition of vulnerability. In particular, we present the battery of health limitations used as the basic metric of a vulnerability condition (extensive margin) as well as the weighting scheme adopted in each country/system in order to aggregate the various dimensions into a single index. We point out how unequal weighting schemes, i.e., the ones which consider some limitations more important than others, often translate into different levels of care needs and, in turn, different levels of benefits or provisions (intensive margin).

We selected countries according to two main criteria: (i) countries characterized by legislations which set a nation-wide or region-wide assessment of need to grant access to care; (ii) countries where a multidisciplinary survey on ageing, containing all the relevant information at the individual level, has been carried out (such as ELSA in England and SHARE in the rest of Europe).

The former criterion lead us to the selection of the following countries: Austria (the cash benefit *Pflegegeld*), Belgium Flanders and Wallonia (the nursing care programme by the *National Institute for Sickness and Disability Insurance*, the cash benefits *Aide à la Personne âgée* and the Flemish *Zorgverzekering*), Germany (the mandatory insurance *Pflegeversicherung*, which was recently reformed and whose rules substantially changed since 2017), France (the programmes *Allocation Personnalisée d'Autonomie* and *Aide ménagère à domicile*), four regional programmes in Italy, Spain (the *Promoción de la Autonomía Personal y Atención a las personas en situación de dependencia*) and the United Kingdom's England and Wales *Social care for Older Adults* programme. These programmes are described in detail in Chap. 3. Unfortunately, the lack of a clear and uniform set of rules prevented us from including in the study of countries such as Denmark (Schulz, 2010), Italy (Da Roit & Le Bihan, 2010; Gori, 2012), the Netherlands (Maarse & Jeurissen, 2016; Mot & Aouragh, 2010), and Sweden (Socialstyrelsen, 2009). Finally, we could not include Scotland for two reasons: first, from the institutional point of view Scotland is a hybrid, since the regulation defines four levels of need-of-care (critical, substantial, moderate, low), where only the first two grant eligibility for care, but, to our knowledge, Scotland does not adopt nation-wide guidelines on how the assessment of need should be performed, so that the criteria are defined at the council level; second, results from the Scottish health survey Healthy Ageing in Scotland (HAGIS) have not yet been released to the scientific community, as its first wave was launched in 2016. The latter selection rule is determined by the nature of our exercise, as we intend to measure on a representative sample of the population the effects of the different LTC systems.

2.2.1 A Broad View on Assessment and Eligibility Rules

Long-term care is typically designed to meet the needs of older individuals who have lost their autonomy, with a significant secondary target of trying to keep them within their domiciliary environment as long as possible. However, the notions of "dependency" or "need-of-care" are heavily based both on the actual limitations experienced by older people and on the assessment-of-need scales.[2]

Table 2.1 summarizes the various dimensions characterizing both the assessment procedures and the minimum eligibility conditions for being granted access to care. The columns "ADL" (activities of daily living) and "iADL" (instrumental activities of daily living) indicate whether these potential limitations are included in the assessment, while the column "Others" includes further vulnerability dimensions, such as cognitive/behavioural problems or advanced self-medication procedures. A separate variable is the application of means-testing, which would consider the economic condition of the applicant or the condition of the household where the applicant lives. Whether or not the information on the provision of informal caregiving affects the eligibility decision is recorded under "informal support": this is a peculiar aspect of some LTC systems which would require as a prerequisite for the benefit provision the presence of a caregiver in the household. The column labelled "eligibility threshold" summarizes how each programme defines the minimum level of objective vulnerability. The last two columns indicate whether the evaluation process gives higher weight to some ADL (including iADL, cognitive and behavioural limitations) in determining the status of loss of autonomy.

As far as the assessment phase is concerned, all the programmes reviewed in this book include some subset of the ADL limitations, together with other limitations in mobility. Many programmes, such as the Austrian, the Czech, the Flemish, the German (before 1 January 2017) and the Spanish, include both the ADL and the iADL; others, such as the Belgian home care programme (INAMI), the reformed German system (since 2017) and the French programmes, do not include iADL in the eligibility criterion, as they want to focus on the "basic limitations", which are obviously more severe. Finally, the Belgian cash-benefit *APA* and the English/Welsh criteria include an incomplete list of both ADL

Table 2.1 LTC programmes in Europe: summary of the relevant criteria

Country	*Program*	*ADL*	*iADL*	*Others*	*Informal support*	*Eligibility threshold*	*Main ADL*	*Main non-ADL*
AT	Pflegegeld	✓	✓	C, S		65 h/month 60 h/month before 2015 50 h/month before 2011	Bathing, dressing, WC	Cooking, housework
BE	APA	P	P	C		7 Points out of 18	–	–
	INAMI/RIZIV (BESADL)	✓		C		Bathing + dressing + moving or using WC/ cognition + bathing + dressing	Bathing, dressing	Cognition
	Vlaamse zorgverzekering (BEL profielschaal)	✓	✓	C		35 Points out of 81	–	Housework, cognition
CZ	Příspěvek na péči	✓	✓	C		3 Deficits out of 10	–	–
DE	Pflegeversicherung pre 2017	✓	✓	C, S		90 m die+/cognition	Bathing, eating, continence	Cognition
	Pflegeversicherung post 2017	✓		C, S		27 Points out of 100	Bathing, eating, WC	Self-post-surgical medications
ES	SAAD	✓	✓	C		25 Points out of 100	Eating, WC	–
FR	APA (AGGIR)	✓*i*		C		2 ADL/cognition	–	Cognition
	Aide ménagère (AGGIR)	✓*i*	P	C		bathing/cooking/housework	Bathing	Cooking, housework
GB(England and Wales)	Social Care for older adults	✓*i*	P	C, M		2 Outcomes	–	–
ITALY								
Bolzano	Assegno di cura (VITA)	✓	✓	C		2 h die		

(*continued*)

Table 2.1 (continued)

Country	*Program*	*ADL*	*iADL*	*Others*	*Informal support*	*Eligibility threshold*	*Main ADL*	*Main non-ADL*
Campania	Assegno di cura (SVaMA)	✓		C,	P	Barthel score 55		
Em. Rom.	Assegno di Cura (BINA)	✓		C, M	✓	230 Points		
Friuli V.G.	CAF/APA (KATZ)	✓		C, M		2 ADL/cognition	–	Cognition
Liguria	ADC (AGED PLUS)	✓	P	C		Invalidity & 3 ADL/ Cognition/Behavior		
Lombardia	Misura B2 (Triage + ADL + iADL)	✓	✓		✓	Invalidity + triage score 3 + 3 ADL + 4 iADL		
Piemonte	Assegno di cura, bonus famiglia (cartella geriatrica)	P	✓	C, B		5 Points		
Sicilia	Buono sociosanit. (SVaMA)	✓	P	M	✓	Invalidity & Living with family		
Toscana	PAC (MDS-HC)	✓*i*		C, B		2 ADL + cognition + behaviour	–	Cognition
Veneto	ICD (SVaMA)	✓		C, M, B	✓	–		

Notes: C cognitive limitations, *M* means tested, *p* included partially, *S* advanced medication for post-surgical conditions, *i* incontinence not included, +Germany: out of the 90 m of need, at least 45 m must come from ADL limitations and iADL, and group them into compound items. Moreover, the English/Welsh assessment evaluates the potential difficulties arising in child-care responsibilities, and it takes into account how functional limitations affect the older person's well-being, which is theoretically conceptualized through a list of subdimensions. The current German system and, to a lower extent, the Austrian system cover a detailed list of advanced self-medication activities, especially related to post-surgical conditions (e.g., catheter/stoma care). Besides ADL and iADL, all programmes include in their assessment of need the deterioration of cognitive and mental abilities[3] to account for the onset of dementia, often together with behavioural risks. On a similar note, some programmes (Austria, Belgium Flanders, the Czech Republic, the current German rules, England/Wales) evaluate how the individual is able to cope with daily planning or to maintain personal relationships.

Several LTC schemes are specifically designed for older people and require a minimum age for eligibility: e.g., 60 years old for the French *APA*, 65 years old for the French *Aide Ménagère* and the Belgian *APA*. Finally, it should be added that all these programmes are *carer-blind*, i.e., they do not include the utilization of informal care (nor its effectiveness) as a condition, while in several countries *means-testing* is implemented, mostly to calibrate the level of the benefit granted to the beneficiary according to the model of a progressive welfare system.

The Italian case is quite complex and it requires a detailed explanation as there exists substantial variability at the regional level or even at the level of municipality or local health unit. Because LTC in Italy appears to be a "patchwork" of schemes, with some areas of the country having low coverage, while others seem quite generous, we restricted our attention to four major regions (or provinces)—Bolzano, Campania, Toscana and Veneto—while briefly commenting on a further six (Emilia-Romagna, Friuli-Venezia Giulia, Liguria, Lombardia, Piemonte and Sicilia). It should be stressed that we do not consider an important cash benefit called *Indennità di Accompagnamento* (IA), which is supposed to pay for caregiving provided within the household by family members. In fact, the assessment-of-need procedure and the eligibility rules for the IA are administered at the local health-council level, thereby making it hard to record all the possible institutional variations and—most importantly—preventing a correct match between each set of rules and individuals in the SHARE-Italian sample with such a fine degree of geocodes. Turning the attention to the other benefit provision, both in-cash and in-kind, they are typically set at the regional level: while all the programmes include in the evaluation cognitive deficits along with the ADL limitations, only some regions also account for limitations in iADL (Bolzano, Lombardia and Piemonte). Utilization of informal caregiving is often part of the assessment protocol in the form of *carer-sighted* evaluation. The inclusion of the presence of a caregiver in the household in the protocol is either aimed at giving priority to beneficiaries living alone (e.g., Lombardia), or to incentivize the effectiveness and adequacy of the care provided. For example, in Sicilia a cash benefit is granted only to older adults who are actually living with family members, while in Veneto the eligibility score of the applicant is higher, the higher the quality of the informal care received. In several regions, such as Veneto, Trentino, Sicilia and Campania, the assessment includes information on clinical diagnosis and complex post-surgical conditions and medications, as well as the housing/neighbourhood environment, even though the minimum eligibility conditions is then determined using a simplified scale which disregards the most detailed clinical information.

In all the countries under investigation the assessment of need is performed by a multidisciplinary team which can include a nurse, a social worker, a doctor, as well as the claimant's relatives or informal caregivers. The team has to review each vulnerability outcome, in order to acknowledge the extent to which the older person can autonomously perform a specific task; a personalized project of care is often planned, which details the patient's entitlement status.

As will become clear in the next chapter, where we will focus on country profiles of LTC coverage, strong heterogeneity exists in the evaluation method adopted by each programme, not only in terms of the dimensions which are included, but also in terms of "scores" attached to the limitation and in terms of "threshold" levels of vulnerability. In Austria and in Bolzano (Italy), but also in Germany pre-2017, each limitation in the assessment-of-need is assigned a nationwide-time amount (hours per month/minutes per day) representing the estimated need-of-care for each specific task where an impediment arises due to limitations.[4] Hence, the eligibility threshold depends on the individual's overall time requirements. For example, in the Spanish system, each limitation carries a specific score between 1 and 100, the score is, in turn, reduced if the individual is only partially limited in a specific task which counts towards the vulnerability condition. The sum of the scores constitutes the overall vulnerability index, and eligibility is granted for values of the index higher than 25. A similar mechanism characterizes the current German system, as well as the Italian system for the regions adopting complex assessment scales as the SVaMA (Campania, Sicilia and Veneto) or the *Cartella Geriatrica* (Piemonte). These protocols involve a large number of outcomes divided into major "vulnerability branches": within each branch, each outcome is assigned a score (depending on the degree of dependence), which is then aggregated into a branch-specific need-score (through a correspondence grid which changes across branches). Summing the need-scores obtained from all branches leads to the overall individual's need-score. In the French AGGIR scale, which is used for both the *APA* and the *Aide Ménagère*, each limitation or item is evaluated on a three-level scale depending on the degree of dependence (full/medium/autonomous) and the eligibility status depends on the specific combination of all possible limitations (and degree of dependence), evaluated through a non-additive algorithm. The three Belgian programmes follow a similar strategy: each item included in the assessment is evaluated on a multiple-value scale (from 0 to 3) according to the severity of the loss of autonomy in each particular task. The Czech's *Příspěvek na péči* as well as England and Wales' *Social Care* and the Italian's Friuli-Venezia Giulia programmes include several items whose evaluation is made on a binary scale (1 = patient is not autonomous/0 = patient is autonomous). The sum of these scores produces an overall vulnerability index, and the loss-of-autonomy status is triggered when the index is higher than a given threshold. Finally, in the Belgian's *INAMI*, the German former *Pflegeversicherung*, the French *APA* and the Italian's Friuli-Venezia Giulia programmes, eligibility can be determined also by significant cognitive impairment and/or behavioural disorders, even when functional limitations are mild.

After having briefly summarized the different systems in terms of the dimensions of vulnerability that are included or excluded from the assessments-of-need protocol, we turn the attention to the evaluation procedure within each scale. We investigate whether some dimensions are relatively more important than others in the determination of a vulnerability level and whether some limitations are necessary and/or sufficient for an individual to reach the minimum eligibility threshold. These are relevant questions as we can show that the significant heterogeneity of rules for access to LTC may strongly discriminate some individuals in one country who, if affected by the same limitations, would be granted the LTC benefit in another country.

An important area of differentiation is the inclusion of mental health in the protocol: in Belgium, Germany, France and Italy cognitive impairments are sufficient conditions for eligibility, even when there are only mild functional limitations. The use of limitation in ADL and/or iADL is another important source of variability: the German system (pre-2017) explicitly indicates that at least one limitation has to occur in each of the two groups of items in order for eligibility to be granted, with the exception of cognitive and mental limitations, which are sufficient conditions for eligibility per se.[5] Similarly, in Bolzano (Italy) the limitations in iADL contribute to the overall vulnerability index only if the ADL limitations are sufficiently serious. The weighting system also generates important differences: in Austria, in Bolzano and in the previous German programme, weights are unequally assigned to the health outcomes included in the assessments of need. More specifically: in the Austrian *Pflegegeld*, losses of autonomy in bathing, dressing and using the toilet are given a higher value (in terms of time requirements) than other ADL; in Germany, the highest weights are given to dependency in bathing and eating, as well as to being incontinent; in Bolzano, the limitations attracting higher weight within the ADL are nutrition and mobility/transferring; in all three programmes, cooking and carrying out household tasks are the most important limitations among the iADL. Of the three Belgian programmes, the APA is the one that gives all its items the same weight, whereas the Flemish insurance scheme allocates higher weights to household- and cognitive-related dimensions,[6] while the assessment scale for the Belgian in-kind home care assistance consider limitations in both washing and dressing as necessary for determining a need-for-LTC. Within the AGGIR scale adopted in France for the *APA* programme, the eligibility condition (category GIR 4) is triggered by the presence of any two ADL items (plus "moving inside the house").[7] The *Aide ménagère* programme, although based on the AGGIR evaluation, has a more general approach since it aims to help older people who have no problems in dressing or moving, but who do need help with washing themselves, or with cooking or with daily tasks as shopping for groceries and small housework. The Spanish SAAD gives different weights to each limitation included in the assessment: in particular, among the ADL limitations, a higher importance is granted to loss of autonomy in eating and in using the toilet. Equal weighting is assigned to the various outcomes in the English/Welsh scheme, in Italy's Friuli-Venezia Giulia and in the Czech Republic.[8] In the current German protocol, each health outcome carries the same weight within a branch, with a few exceptions such as limitations in washing, eating or using the toilet. However, highly different relative weights are applied to the different branches when computing the overall final vulnerability score: e.g., 40% to the ADL limitations branch, 15% to the Depression and the Cognition loss branches. In those Italian regions which adopt the Barthel ADL scale (Campania, Piemonte and Veneto), higher weight is given to limitations in mobility.

Notes

1. As LaPlante (2010) highlights, the ADL scale embeds a paediatric model: "as a child matures, the simplest activity, eating, is mastered first, then continence, transferring, toileting, dressing, and bathing, in order of increasing complexity". As a person ages, functional losses occur in the reverse order. On the hierarchical structure of ADL and iADL see also Wiener, Hanley, Clark, and Van Nostrand (1990), Kempen, Myers, and Powell (1995) and Thomas, Rockwood, and McDowell (1998).
2. We focus the attention on older people because in this book we are addressing the challenges of an ageing population, however some programmes do not require a specific age in order to become eligible for care.
3. France adopts the same assessment tool (AGGIR scale) for both the LTC programmes considered here. The presence of cognitive impairment determines eligibility to the APA programme.
4. In both programmes, the regulation provides nationwide fixed guidelines to ensure comparability in the evaluation across different areas of the country.
5. This rule was introduced with the 2012 reform (Law on Realignment of Care/*Pflege-Neuausrichtungs-Gesetz*).
6. Although each single item has equal weight on the BEL scale, the household-management and the cognitive/mental tasks are more numerous and detailed, thus resulting in a higher weight allocated to these two dimensions of vulnerability.
7. The outcome "moving inside the house" is not a sufficient limitation for eligibility when the only other loss-of autonomy concerns the "transferring" task, but it is when at least one among "using the toilet", "dressing", "eating" or "washing" is present.
8. The Czech assessment-of-need accumulates some ADL or iADL in the same scale-item. Some unequal weighting, with respect to the ADL and iADL, could therefore arise between those tasks that are compounded together in a single item with those who are not, since each item in the Czech scale has the same weight regardless of it being a compound or not.

References

Bakx, P., Meijer, C., Schut, F., & Doorslaer, E. (2014). Going formal or informal, who cares? The influence of public long-term care insurance. *Health Economics, 24*, 631–643. https://doi.org/10.1002/hec.3050

Brock, D. W. (1989). *Quality of life measures in health care and medical ethics*. Working Paper No. 66, World Institute for Development Economics Research of the United Nations University.

Clegg, A., Young, J., Iliffe, S., Rikkert, M. O., & Rockwood, K. (2013). Frailty in elderly people. *The Lancet, 381*(9868), 752–762.

Colombo, F., & Mercier, J. (2012). Help wanted? Fair and sustainable financing of long-term care services. *Applied Economic Perspectives and Policy, 34*(2), 316–332.

Comas-Herrera, A., Costa-i-Font, J., Gori, C., di Maio, A., Patxot, C., Pickard, L., … Wittenberg, R. (2003). *European study of long-term care expenditure: Investigating the sensitivity of projections of future long-term care expenditure in Germany, Spain, Italy and the United Kingdom to changes in assumptions about demography, dependency, informal care, formal care and unit costs*. Report to the European Commission, Employment & Social Affairs DG. PSSRU Discussion Paper 1840.

Conroy, S. (2009). Defining frailty—The holy grail of geriatric medicine. *The Journal of Nutrition, Health & Aging, 13*(4), 389–389.

Da Roit, B., & Le Bihan, B. (2010). Similar and yet so different: Cash-for-care in six European countries' long-term care policies. *Milbank Quarterly, 88*(3), 286–309.

De Vries, N., Staal, J., Van Ravensberg, C., Hobbelen, J., Olde Rikkert, M., & Nijhuis-Van der Sanden, M. (2011). Outcome instruments to measure frailty: A systematic review. *Ageing Research Reviews, 10*(1), 104–114.

Eleftheriades, C., & Wittenberg, R. (2013). *A critical review of international practice on assessment and eligibility in adult social care: Lessons for England*. Oxford: Centre for Health Service Economics & Organisation (CHSEO).

European Commission. (2015). *The 2015 Ageing Report*. Luxembourg: Publications Office of the European Union.

Fried, L. P., Ferrucci, L., Darer, J., Williamson, J. D., & Anderson, G. (2004). Untangling the concepts of disability, frailty, and comorbidity: Implications for improved targeting and care. *The Journals of Gerontology Series A: Biological Sciences and Medical Sciences, 59*(3), M255–M263.

Fulop, T., Larbi, A., Witkowski, J. M., McElhaney, J., Loeb, M., Mitnitski, A., & Pawelec, G. (2010). Aging, frailty and age-related diseases. *Biogerontology, 11*(5), 547–563.

Gallagher, A., Li, S., Wainwright, P., Jones, I. R., & Lee, D. (2008). Dignity in the care of older people—A review of the theoretical and empirical literature. *BMC Nursing, 7*(1), 11.

Gori, C. (2012). Home care in Italy: A system on the move, in the opposite direction to what we expect. *Health & Social Care in the Community, 20*(3), 255–264.

Gori, C., & Fernandez, J.-L. (2015). *Long-term care reforms in OECD countries*. Bristol: Policy Press.

Jiménez-Martín, S., & Prieto, C. V. (2010). A double sample selection model for unmet needs, formal care and informal caregiving hours of dependent people in Spain. *Documento de Trabajo, 2010*, 25.

Katz, S., Downs, T. D., Cash, H. R., & Grotz, R. C. (1970). Progress in development of the index of ADL. *The Gerontologist, 10*(1 Part 1), 20–30. https://doi.org/10.1093/geront/10.1_Part_1.20

Kempen, G. I. J. M., Myers, A. M., & Powell, L. E. (1995). Hierarchical structure in ADL and IADL: Analytical assumptions and applications for clinicians and researchers. *Journal of Clinical Epidemiology, 48*(11), 1299–1305. https://doi.org/10.1016/0895-4356(95)00043-7

LaPlante, M. P. (2010). The classic measure of disability in activities of daily living is biased by age but an expanded IADL/ADL measure is not. *The Journals of Gerontology Series B: Psychological Sciences and Social Sciences, 65*(6), 720–732. https://doi.org/10.1093/geronb/gbp129.

Lawton, M. P., & Brody, E. M. (1969). Assessment of older people: Self-maintaining and instrumental activities of daily living. *The Gerontologist, 9*(3), 179–186.

Maarse, J. A. M., & Jeurissen, P. P. (2016). The policy and politics of the 2015 long-term care reform in the Netherlands. *Health Policy, 120*(3), 241–245. https://doi.org/10.1016/j.healthpol.2016.01.014

Mahoney, F., & Barthel, D. (1965). Functional evaluation: The Barthel Index. *Maryland State Medical Journal, 14*, 61.

Markle-Reid, M., & Browne, G. (2003). Conceptualizations of frailty in relation to older adults. *Journal of Advanced Nursing, 44*(1), 58–68.

Mitnitski, A. B., Mogilner, A. J., & Rockwood, K. (2001). Accumulation of deficits as a proxy measure of aging. *The Scientific World Journal, 1*, 323–336.

Mot, E., & Aouragh, A. (2010). *The Dutch system of long-term care*. ENEPRI.

Nordenfelt, L. (2004). The varieties of dignity. *Health Care Analysis, 12*(2), 69–81. https://doi.org/10.1023/B:HCAN.0000041183.78435.4b.

Nussbaum, M., & Sen, A. (1993). *The quality of life*. Oxford University Press.

OECD. (2013). *A good life in old age?* Paris: OECD Publishing.

Pel-Littel, R., Schuurmans, M., Emmelot-Vonk, M., & Verhaar, H. (2009). Frailty: Defining and measuring of a concept. *JNHA—The Journal of Nutrition, Health and Aging, 13*(4), 390–394.

Pialoux, T., Goyard, J., & Lesourd, B. (2012). Screening tools for frailty in primary health care: A systematic review. *Geriatrics & Gerontology International, 12*(2), 189–197.

Pilotto, A., & Ferrucci, L. (2011). Verso una definizione clinica della fragilità: utilità dell'approccio multidimensionale. *Giornale di Gerontologia*, *59*, 125–129.

Pilotto, A., Gallina, P., Fontana, A., Sancarlo, D., Bazzano, S., Copetti, M., … Pellegrini, F. (2013). Development and validation of a Multidimensional Prognostic Index for mortality based on a standardized multidimensional assessment schedule (MPI-SVaMA) in community-dwelling older subjects. *Journal of the American Medical Directors Association*, *14*(4), 287–292.

Rockwood, K., & Mitnitski, A. (2007). Frailty in relation to the accumulation of deficits. *The Journals of Gerontology Series A: Biological Sciences and Medical Sciences*, *62*(7), 722–727.

Rodríguez-Mañas, L., Féart, C., Mann, G., Viña, J., Chatterji, S., Chodzko-Zajko, W., … Nicholson, C. (2013). Searching for an operational definition of frailty: A delphi method based consensus statement. The frailty operative definition-consensus conference project. *The Journals of Gerontology Series A: Biological Sciences and Medical Sciences*, *68*(1), 62–67.

Schulz, E. (2010). *The long-term care system in Denmark*. ENEPRI Research Report No. 73, 28 May.

Socialstyrelsen. (2009). *Care of older people in Sweden 2008*. Socialstyrelsen—National Board of Health and Welfare.

Sourial, N., Wolfson, C., Bergman, H., Zhu, B., Karunananthan, S., Quail, J., … Béland, F. (2010). A correspondence analysis revealed frailty deficits aggregate and are multidimensional. *Journal of Clinical Epidemiology*, *63*(6), 647–654.

Thomas, V. S., Rockwood, K., & McDowell, I. (1998). Multidimensionality in instrumental and basic activities of daily living. *Journal of Clinical Epidemiology*, *51*(4), 315–321.

WHO. (2002). *Towards a common language for functioning, disability and health*. Geneva: World Health Organization. Retrieved from http://www.who.int/classifications/icf/en/

Wiener, J. M., Hanley, R. J., Clark, R., & Van Nostrand, J. F. (1990). Measuring the activities of daily living: Comparisons across national surveys. *Journal of Gerontology*, *45*(6), S229–S237.

CHAPTER 3

Country Profiles of Eligibility Legislations in Europe

Abstract In this chapter, we detail the main LTC legislations in Austria, Belgium, the Czech Republic, England, France, Germany, Italy and Spain. Each country profile includes up-to-date legislative information, details on the assessment of need procedures, the eligibility rules and the in-kind or in-cash benefits for the eligible population. The chapters for Belgium and Italy are organised at the regional level, given the high degree of heterogeneity of the local LTC programmes.

Keywords Long-term care legislation • LTC benefits • Regional programmes

This chapter offers details on the major European programmes of home-based care for older adults in Europe. The countries covered are Austria, Belgium, the Czech Republic, France, Germany, Spain, the United Kingdom (England and Wales), and four Italian regions (see Chap. 2 for an overall comparison).

We organise the presentation by devoting a paragraph to each country and then review, in a systematic way, the impact of the different rules on the population at risk of vulnerability. In particular, we match the assessment-of-need scales and the eligibility rules of each country or region with the actual information collected at the individual level by the SHARE and ELSA surveys (also referred to as the "dataset").[1] The aim

A. Brugiavini et al., *Vulnerability and Long-term Care in Europe*,
https://doi.org/10.1007/978-3-319-68969-2_3

of this exercise is to eventually simulate how the legal benchmark and the protocol of each country generates a given level of coverage for home-based care. While the actual econometric exercise of estimating the coverage for each country and performing counterfactual exercises is the topic of Chap. 4, in this chapter we simply report, side by side, the legal framework (left column) and the corresponding information contained in SHARE or ELSA (right column). This matching exercise is carried out in a prudent and robust fashion, in order to identify a sub-population of eligible individuals in the sample: we are fully aware of the fact that we cannot replicate the actual granting procedure and mimic the work and the expertise of the trained professionals who perform the assessments in the field. However, SHARE and ELSA are the ideal datasets to carry out this kind of exercise, as nearly all the dimensions included in the protocols have a close correspondent in the dataset at the individual level, either in the form of a self-reported item (such as limitations in ADL) or as an objective measure. However, some adjustments in the survey data have to be made in order to guarantee full comparability, as will be detailed in Chap. 4. To the extent that there is a measurement error in our matching procedure, this should be "neutral", i.e., it should not systematically produce estimates with higher (or lower) rates of take-up.

3.1 The Austrian *Pflegegeld*

The Austrian legislation for the LTC-benefit programme (*Pflegegeld*) does not indicate a direct medical definition of *vulnerability*, but it does include a profile of a person-in-need: "an individual who needs frequent help from others in tasks that primarily affect their personal lives, and who would be seriously exposed in everyday life without that support".[2]

Eligibility is based on individual requirements of care and its assessment-of-need follows a uniform federal set of guidelines defined by the Regulations on the Classification of the need of care (*Einstufungsverordnung*[3]) related to the Federal Long-term-care Act (*Bundes-pflegegeld-gesetzes*[4]). Austrian older adults can be granted the allowance upon a legal entitlement in the form of LTC insurance, regardless of their income, age and the cause of their limitation. They also have a high degree of freedom in the usage of the benefit, which is tax-free, for financing their long-term care services, although the allowance can be converted into an in-kind benefit in case of improper use of the money.[5]

The assessment of need covers a wide number of potential functioning limitations (ADL and iADL), together with a specific formalisation of a potential need-of-care for post-surgery conditions or complex auto-medication. What is peculiar to this vulnerability assessment is that each limitation is converted in a specific amount of time, measured in terms of hours per month. Each benchmark is, indeed, the minimum amount of care that—the law assumes—should be needed by a patient suffering from that deficit. Table 3.1 lists the dimensions of vulnerability together with their respective allotted minimum amount of care.

A few points are worth stressing here, with regard to the *Pflegegeld* assessment-of-need. A first inspection of the table suggests that vulnerability is based on difficulties on a number of tasks, which are mainly divided in two groups: *core* and *auxiliary* activities (*Betreuungs-Maßnahmen* and *Hilfs-Verrichtungen*). The first category coincides partially with the Activities of Daily Living as defined by Katz, which are all individually assessed in the screening. The tasks related to *going to the toilet* and *eating* have a benchmark time of care of 30 hours per month each (1 hour per day), as it is for the *meals preparation* activity (which belongs to the iADL list by Lawton). *Daily body care* is supposed to take 25 hours per month (two times a day, 25 minutes each) while the time given for *dressing and undressing* is estimated in 20 hours per month (two times a day, 20 minutes each). If an individual suffers from incontinence, additional time is allotted (20 hours a month, four times a day with 10 minutes each) for performing hygiene tasks. With regard to the *mobility* task, the Austrian Regulation includes the assessment of the need for *in-house mobility* help, encompassing both the *Transferring* task from the ADL (moving in and out of bed or chair unassisted) and the broader activity of moving inside one's own house or apartment. *Taking medications* (one of Lawton's iADL) is included as a core activity and requires 3 hours per month (6 minutes per day). It refers to the ability to properly prepare and self-administer medications, injections and inhalations, including the task of remembering the intake schedule. The last four tasks included in the screening are much more specific than the ones listed before, and relates to specific medications or procedures, and to a population who had undergone specific medical surgery. These tasks involve activities such as self-administered enemas (15 hours per month, 30 minutes per day), care and maintenance of a tracheal cannula, a gastric tube (5 hours per month, 10 minutes per day), a catheter (5 hours per month, 10 minutes per day) or an artificial anus (7.5 hours per month, 15 minutes per day).

Table 3.1 Austrian *Pflegegeld* assessment-of-need and the SHARE data

Core/auxiliary	*Limitation*	*Fixed need-of-care (hours/month)*	*SHARE tasks (binary: yes/no)*
c	Daily body care	25	Bathing or showering
c	Preparation of meals	30	Preparing a hot meal
c	Taking meals	30	Eating (+ cutting up your food)
c	Defecation	30	Using the toilet (+ getting up or down)
c	Dressing and undressing	20	Dressing (+ putting on shoes and socks)
c	Cleaning for incontinence sufferers	20	Incontinence or involuntary loss of urine
c	Colostomy care	7.5	–
c	Care cannula tube care	5	–
c	Catheter care	5	–
c	Enemas	15	–
c	Taking medication	3	Taking medications
c	Mobility aid in the narrow sense	15	Walking across a room *or* Getting in or out of bed
a	Motivational talks	10	EURO-D scale
a	Emptying and cleaning the toilet chair	10	–
a	Procuring of food and medicines	10	Shopping for groceries
a	Cleaning the home and personal effects	10	Doing work around the house
a	Care of underwear and towels	10	Doing work around the house
a	Heating the living space (+procuring of fuel)	10	Doing work around the house
a	Mobility aid in a broader sense	10	Using a map to figure out how to get around in a strange place
	Cognitive impairment[a]	25[a]	Disoriented in time (day, week, month, year): Cannot answer three or more

Gesamte Rechtsvorschrift für Einstufungsverordnung zum Bundespflegegeldgesetz, BGBl. II Nr. 37/1999, BGBl. II Nr. 453/2011

[a]Since 1 January 2009

Alongside the core activities the screening comprises seven *auxiliary* tasks, which principally refer to the Lawton's Instrumental ADL such as housework (*cleaning the household*, *doing laundry* and *heating the living space*), *shopping for groceries or medicines* and *moving outside the house*. An additional dimension is comprised to account for the potential difficulties of those who use a toilet chair, and assigns 10 hours of -care per month for those unable to empty and clean their chair. Finally, *motivational talks*, which target those with mental or spiritual (*sic*) limitations who need help in planning their daily activities in order to live an active and independent living, can account for 10 hours per month. Since 1 January 2009, people with mental illnesses, dementia or severe behavioural disorders are allocated a fixed supplementary amount of care-time in terms of 25 hours per month.[6]

As a last note, the assessment of need described above builds a *weighted* measure of vulnerability, since each dimension that contributes to the definition of the dependency status is weighted throughout the amount of hours of need requested for that specific limitation. This results, as an example, in a difficulty related to nutrition (*taking meals*, 30 hours per month) having a double weight with respect to *mobility limitations* (15 hours per month) in defining vulnerability. From the list of activities shown above, it is easy to see how the *core activities* are generally weighted more than the *auxiliary* ones, in line with the point often made by geriatricians, that limitations in ADL play a key role in making an individual vulnerable.

Since 2016, a care allowance is paid to individuals who present a general decline in functional status that requires at least 65 hours of need-of-care per month and is expected to last for at least 6 months due to a physical, mental or emotional disability or sensory impairment in *at least one* core activity and *at least one* auxiliary activity.[7] The cash benefit is paid through 12 monthly instalments, for a whole year, and the monthly amount depends on the patient's level of need. The allowance is paid directly to the person in need, without any obligation to pay for care or to use care services (OECD Health Statistics 2014). Although the minimum amount of need is currently 65 hours per month (out of a maximum of 275.5), which allows for a monthly benefit of €157, vulnerable older persons are offered higher benefits as long as their demand-for-care grows, up to a maximum of € 1.689. Indeed, seven levels of eligibility are defined by law, as summarised in Table 3.2.

Table 3.2 Austrian *Pflegegeld* eligibility rules

Level	*Need-of-care per month for at least one core and one auxiliary task*	*Allowance € per month (2017)*
I	At least 65 h (60 h before 2016, 50 h before 2011)	157.30
II	At least 90 h (85 h before 2016, 75 h before 2011)	290.00
III	At least 120 h	451.80
IV	At least 160 h	677.60
V	At least 180 h of care needed per month, if an unusual need for LTC is required.	920.30
VI	At least 180 h of care needed per month, if (1) care measures are required, which cannot be coordinated in terms of time and these are provided on a regular basis during day and night or (2) the continuous presence of a care giver is required during day and night, because it is probable that there is a danger for the care recipient of for other persons.	1285.20
VII	At least 180 h of care needed per month, if (1) it is not possible for the four extremities to move intentionally or (2) a similar situation occurs.	1688.90

Updated from Riedel and Kraus (2010), BMASK (2013b)

In order to be granted the cash benefit, an application must be submitted to the competent social insurance institution, i.e., the one that pays the pension or annuity to the patient (*Pensionsversicherungs-Anstalt, die Versicherungsanstalt öffentlich Bediensteter, die Sozialversicherungsanstalt der Bauern*). Those who are not in receipt of any pension should submit the application to the Pension Insurance Institute. After the application is filed, an appointment is scheduled for an in-house assessment-of-need,[8] which is usually performed by a doctor and a nurse specialist together with the applicant and a trusted third person, who might cooperate in giving information about the type of care required. When necessary, other professionals from different fields (Social Service, Psychology, Psychotherapy) can be involved in the evaluation. Once the applicant is regarded eligible and the amount of the allowance is set, the allowance is paid retroactively starting from the month in which the application was submitted. If the applicant does not agree with the decision, either because she has been excluded from the care allowance or because she believes she deserves a higher allowance, an appeal can be filed to the Labour and Social Court.

3.2 The Belgian System

3.2.1 *Belgian Home Nursing Care (INAMI/RIZIV)*

Home nursing care in Belgium is reimbursed by the National Institute for Sickness and Disability Insurance (*Institut National d'Assurance Maladie-Invalidité/Rijksinstituut voor Zieke en Invaliditeitsverzekering*—INAMI/RIZIV), which is responsible for the general organisation and financial management of the federal compulsory public health insurance.[9,10] As described in Sermeus et al. (2010), "its most important tasks are to prepare and implement legislation and regulation, to prepare the budget, to monitor the evolution of health care spending, to control whether legislation and regulation are correctly implemented by health care providers and sickness funds and to organise the consultation between the different actors involved in the compulsory health insurance" (Table 3.3).

Benefits in-kind, i.e., formal home nursing care, are provided irrespective of the patients' age or income and based solely on their vulnerability conditions. The degree of reimbursement and the method of payment (fee-for-service or lump-sum payment) depend on the applicant's degree of dependency. As a tool for the assessment of need, NIHDI adopted an ADL scale,[11] slightly adapted from the Katz taxonomy, which includes six items on functioning and two on mental coherence and orientation. The applicant's dependency or need-of-care for each item scores on a four-step scale for each item (from 1 to 4), where 0 corresponds to full autonomy and 4 corresponds to finding it impossible to perform the specific task. Dependency status on a single item arises when the need-of-care is either severe (3) or full (4).

When we will implement these rules on SHARE data (Chap. 4), we will prudentially assign the score of 3 whenever a respondent reports to suffer from a limitation in the specific task, as Table 3.4 illustrates.

Three main categories of dependency are established by the NIHDI. The minimum eligible level of vulnerability corresponds to level B of the vulnerability scale, and refers to two profiles: (i) being limited in bathing and dressing *and* in moving *or* going to the toilet; (ii) being disoriented in time and space *and* being limited in bathing and dressing (INAMI, 2016; Karakaya, 2009; Sermeus et al., 2010).

As detailed in Sermeus et al. (2010), low-dependency patients (category A) are reimbursed through fee-for-service related payments. With

Table 3.3 Belgian assessment of need for home nursing care

Criteria	*Score 1*	*Score 2*	*Score 3*	*Score 4*
Bathing	Able to wash him/herself without help	Needs assistance in washing above or below the waist	Needs assistance in washing above and below waist	Must be fully supported in washing
Dressing	Able to dress and undress without help	Needs assistance to dress above or below the waist (excluding laces)	Needs assistance to dress above and below the waist	Must be fully supported in dressing above and below the waist
Moving and transferring	Autonomous in moving and transferring without help or appliances	Autonomous in moving and transferring, using appliances	Need help for at least one move or transfer	Bedridden or in wheelchair, fully dependent to move and transfer
Using the toilet	Able to use the toilet, including (un)dressing and cleaning, without help	Needs help for one among: Going to the toilet, dressing, cleaning	Needs help for two among: going to the toilet, dressing, cleaning	Needs help in going to the toilet, dressing and cleaning
Continence	Able to retain urine and stool	Accidentally incontinent for urine or stool[a]	Incontinent for urine or stool	Incontinent for urine and stool
Eating	Able to eat and drink independently	Needs help before eating or drinking	Needs some assistance while eating or drinking	Totally dependent for eating or drinking
Orientation in time	No limitations	Seldom problems	Frequent problems	Completely disoriented
Orientation in space	No limitations	Seldom problems	Frequent problems	Completely disoriented

Source: Sermeus et al. (2010)

[a]Including patients with urinary catheter or artificial anus

the exception of hygienic nursing care, a doctor's prescription is required for the reimbursement of all nursing interventions in the fee-for-service payment system. Beneficiaries falling into the category B or C/Cdement are reimbursed through per diem lump sums, a type of fee-for-service payment system based on the number of days of care. A doctor's prescription is not required for reimbursement of nursing care delivery under the lump-sum system, except for technical interventions under fee-for-service

Table 3.4 Belgian nursing home-care programme and SHARE

Criteria	*Value assigned in SHARE*	*SHARE tasks (binary: yes/no)*
Bathing	3 out of 4	Bathing or showering
Dressing	3 out of 4	Dressing (+ putting on shoes and socks)
Moving and transferring	3 out of 4	Walking across a room *or* Getting in or out of bed
Using the toilet	3 out of 4	Using the toilet (+ getting up or down)
Continence	3 out of 4	Incontinence or involuntary loss of urine
Eating	3 out of 4	Eating (+ cutting up your food)
Orientation in time	3 out of 4	Disoriented in time (day, week, month, year): Cannot answer three or more
Orientation in space	3 out of 4	Disoriented in time (day, week, month, year): Cannot answer three or more

such as injections, wound care, bladder care, gastro-intestinal care, specific technical nursing interventions). Additional per diem lump sums apply to palliative care and diabetic patient (Table 3.5).

3.2.2 The Belgian APA

The main **Belgian** LTC cash benefit, the Assistance to Older People (APA: *Aide à la Personne âgée*), allows eligible dependent individuals to benefit from an allowance whose amount is primarily based on a vulnerability evaluation.[12] Besides the applicant's health status, eligibility is based on a series of socio-demographic criteria including age, marital status and family composition. Moreover, the programme is means-tested since household income is taken into account in determining the monetary amount of the benefit. Until the end of 2016 the APA was managed at the federal level for all Belgians, regardless of their region. Since 1 January 2017, the competence of the APA has been transferred to the Flemish Community for all inhabitants of Flanders.[13]

The assessment process is performed through a scale (APA scale) which depicts vulnerability as determined by six items that are briefly described in Table 3.6.

Each item is evaluated on a scale from 0 (no difficulties in performing the selected item) to 3 (impossibility in performing the selected item without help from others), and the overall profile of vulnerability is constructed by summing each item' scores. When we will match the APA scale to the

Table 3.5 Belgian eligibility rules for home nursing care

Category	*Physical dependence*		*Mental dependence*
O	No dependence	AND	No dependence
A	Dependent in bathing and dressing	OR	Disoriented in time and space (but physically independent)
B	Dependent in bathing and dressing, AND dependent for moving and/or going to the toilet	OR	Disoriented in time and space, AND dependent in bathing and/or dressing
C	Dependent in bathing and dressing, AND dependent for moving and going to the toilet AND dependent for incontinence and/or eating	AND	No dependence
Cdement	As in category C	AND	Disoriented in time and space

Source: Sermeus et al. (2010)

Table 3.6 Belgian's APA assessment of need

Limitations	*Value*	*SHARE tasks*	*Value assigned in SHARE*
Moving and transferring around the house	0–3	Walking across a room *or* Getting in or out of bed	2 out of 3
Preparing meals and ingesting food	0–3	Preparing a hot meal *or* Eating (+ cutting up your food)	2 out of 3
Performing body care and being able to dress	0–3	Bathing/showering *or* Dressing (+ putting on shoes and socks)	2 out of 3
Taking care of own house and performing household tasks	0–3	Doing work around the house *or* Managing money, such as paying bills and keeping track of expenses	2 out of 3
Communication: being able to have contacts with others	0–3	Making telephone calls	2 out of 3
Need of supervision: being able to assess and avoid dangerous situations	0–3	Disoriented in time (day, week, month, year): Cannot answer three or more	2 out of 3
Minimum age required for eligibility: 65 year old			

Source: Royal Decree (Arrêté royal), 5 March 1990

SHARE data, we will assign the score of 2 whenever a respondent reports to suffer from a limitation included in the assessment.

The highest possible level of dependency in the APA scale is represented by a score of 18. The minimum level of vulnerability corresponds to a score of 7: if an applicant receives an overall index of less than 7 they are ineligible for the monetary allowance. Additional socio-economic criteria must be fulfilled in order to be granted the benefit. With regard to demographic characteristics, an individual must be at least 65 years old and being of Belgian nationality or a foreign resident to apply for the programme. Furthermore, the allowance is differentiated in five categories which depend on the patient's health status: scores of 7 and 8 give entitlement to category allowance 1, scores of 9 and 11 to category allowance 2, scores of 12 and 14 to category 3, scores of 15 or 16 to category 4, while a score higher than 16 corresponds to category allowance 5. The cash benefits in Euro vary from €981.68 per year (category 1) to €6589.77 per year (category 5), and are inflation-indexed.

After determining the vulnerability category of the applicant, means-testing is performed on a household's income in order to determine the actual monetary amount to be granted by the APA programme. The income test takes into account the household composition and the marital status of the applicant. No allowance reduction is applied to those who live alone or with other family members and have zero income or anyway an annual income lower than €12,672.36. Similarly, for those who live with a partner who is not part of the family, no reductions will be applied up to an overall yearly income ceiling (of the applicant and his/her partner) of €15,835.19. The law specifies which sources of income are included in (or excluded from) the test. As an example, the means-test includes pensions, real estates, savings and financial assets. Table 3.7 provides the maximum amounts (no reductions) corresponding to each category:[14]

The assessment process follows several steps. A preliminary application must be submitted in the local municipality, a series of forms must then be filled in by the applicant and his/her family doctor, with personal data and a brief self-evaluation of applicant's own dependency status. After returning these files to the Federal Social Services Department, an appointment with a doctor will be scheduled (the appointed can be arranged at the patient's home, would he be unable to move outside) and the official evaluation of the vulnerability condition will take place. The assessment formalises the extent to which the applicant's limitations affect his/her ability to conduct the usual daily activities of an independent life, and

Table 3.7 Belgian APA eligibility rules

Category	*Maximum allocation amount in € (2017) per year (inflation-indexed)*
Category 1 (7–8 points)	1001.32
Category 2 (9–11 points)	3822.28
Category 3 (12–14 points)	4647.27
Category 4 (15–16 points)	5472.03
Category 5 (17–18 points)	6721.61
Age requirement: 65 or older	

Source: FPS Social Security, http://handicap.belgium.be/fr/mes-droits/allocation-aide-personnes-agees.htm

whether these limitations are permanent or are subjected to evolve (worsening or improving) in the future. Should the latter be true, a new assessment in the forthcoming months will be scheduled in order to keep track of the patient's conditions and, if needed, to make the necessary modifications to his/her eligible status with respect to the APA benefit. Based on the medical evaluation, the final decision about the applicant's eligibility rests with the Service Department. In case of disagreement, the applicant can file an appeal to the Labour Court (*Arbeidsrechtbank/Tribunal du travail*) no more than three months after the decision has been notified.

The APA scale presents several peculiarities that are worth stressing. It is a relatively short scale (six items), and yet it encompasses more than six functional limitations, since there are items which aggregate pairs of activities and even mixtures of ADL and iADL. The "moving" item comprises both the "moving around the house" and the "transferring" tasks, while there is a single domain "bathing and dressing" which considers together the ability of performing body care and of dressing/undressing. The "nutrition" item evaluates both the patient's ability to prepare a meal (which is an iADL) and the ability to ingest and cutting up the food (which is an ADL).[15] Other iADL-related tasks are also included in the assessment: the ability to perform house-tasks and ability to entertain contacts with others.[16] The last component of the APA scale is quite wide and generically defined, since it involves the "ability to recognise and avoid dangers". The latter is an ability that may entail both cognitive and mental limitations (being able to recognise the presence or the potential occurrence of a danger) together with physical limitations (ability to recognise a danger, i.e., ability to see or hear the preliminary stages of a dangerous situation, or ability to avoid a danger, i.e., ability to move away from a location or ability to perform proper self-medications). Other ADL limitations, such as incontinence or ability to use the toilet, are not explicitly considered, although the latter could be partially spotted in the "moving" and in the "bathing and dressing" items. Numerous other iADL are excluded from the APA evaluation of vulnerability, like shopping for groceries, performing self-medications, moving outside their own house, and handling finances.

Each item is perfectly substitutable to the others in contributing to the vulnerability index and each item has the same weight (i.e., no item-specific weights are specified, the overall score is just the sum of each item' score). It is more difficult to infer the weights assigned to single ADL/iADL tasks considered in the APA scale, since they are lumped together into a unique item.

Finally, as already mentioned, the evaluation of the limitation degree for a single item is multivariate, and spans from a minimum score of 0 (no limitation is present) to 3 (impossibility to perform the activities described in the item), and therefore requires a higher precision than the assessment based on a binary evaluation (0/1).

3.2.3 The Flemish Zorgverzekering

The Belgian **Flemish** region envisages a care-allowance that is part of a separate LTC insurance scheme (*Zorgverzekering*/Care Insurance)[17] with respect to the nationwide APA and the home-care programme, discussed in Sects. 3.2.2 and 3.2.1 above. Vulnerability is assessed on a detailed evaluation scale (BEL scale BEL-profielschaal) that assigns a dependency score to each applicant. Eligibility is limited to Flemish and Brussels-Capital population, it is neither age-related nor income-related, but it requires that the minimum BEL score be higher than a fixed threshold (35 points). The cash benefit has a fixed amount of €130, irrespective of the patient's need-of-care.

The BEL scale (*BEL-foto*) identifies 27 vulnerability outcomes to be assessed, split in four domains (dimensions), namely *household-related activities*, *physical activities*, *social-related activities* and *mental health issues*. Each of the 27 tasks has to be evaluated on a four-step scale (from 0 to 3), where 0 corresponds to full autonomy and 3 corresponds to impossibility to perform the specific task. The sum of each task score provides the patient's dependency index. The highest achievable overall value is 81 (i.e., a patient that has full need-of-care in each of the 27 tasks).

Table 3.8 summarises the 4 dimensions of the BEL scale and their related tasks. When matching these rules to the SHARE data, since most

Table 3.8 Belgian Flanders LTC assessment of need and the SHARE data

Limitation	*Value*	*SHARE tasks (binary: yes/no)*	*Value assigned in SHARE*
Household ADL			
Householding	0–3	Doing work around the house	2 out of 3
Laundry	0–3	Doing work around the house	2 out of 3
Ironing	0–3	Doing work around the house	2 out of 3
Shopping	0–3	Shopping for groceries	2 out of 3
Meal preparation	0–3	Preparing a hot meal	2 out of 3
Housework planning	0–3	Doing work around the house	2 out of 3
Physical ADL			
Bathing and showering	0–3	Bathing or showering	2 out of 3
Dressing	0–3	Dressing (+ putting on shoes and socks)	2 out of 3
Functional mobility	0–3	Getting in or out of bed	2 out of 3
Using the toilet	0–3	Using the toilet (+ getting up or down)	2 out of 3
Incontinence	0–3	Incontinence or involuntary loss of urine	2 out of 3
Feeding	0–3	Eating (+ cutting up your food)	2 out of 3
Social ADL			
Social loss	0–3	EURO-D scale = 4 or higher	2 out of 3
Commitment to therapy and medical rules	0–3	Taking medications	2 out of 3
Safety inside/outside the house	0–3	Doing work around the house or garden	2 out of 3
Administration	0–3	Managing money, such as paying bills and keeping track of expenses	2 out of 3
Financial operations	0–3	Managing money, such as paying bills and keeping track of expenses	2 out of 3
Mental health			
Orientation in time	0–3	Disoriented in time (day, week, month, year): Cannot answer three or more	2 out of 3
Orientation in space	0–3	Disoriented in time (day, week, month, year): Cannot answer three or more	2 out of 3

(*continued*)

Table 3.8 (continued)

Limitation	*Value*	*SHARE tasks (binary: yes/no)*	*Value assigned in SHARE*
Orientation in persons	0–3	–	
Purposeless behaviour	0–3	EURO-D scale = 4 or higher	2 out of 3
Disruptive behaviour	0–3	EURO-D scale = 4 or higher	2 out of 3
Lack of initiative	0–3	EURO-D scale = 4 or higher	2 out of 3
Depressed mood	0–3	EURO-D scale = 4 or higher	2 out of 3
Anxious mood	0–3	EURO-D scale = 4 or higher	2 out of 3

Evaluation for each item: 0—no need-of-care; 1—small need-of-care; 2—medium need-of-care; 3—full need-of-care

Source: Second Annex to the Ministerial Decree of 6 January 2006 regulating the determination of the severity and duration of the reduced autonomy on the basis of the BEL-profielschaal under the Flemish care insurance

of the health-conditions in the survey are reported on a binary scale (yes/no),[18] we assign a score of 2 in the BEL scale to each reported limitation in the sample. Moreover, we take a prudential approach in defining the Mental Health conditions related to purposeless/disruptive behaviours, lack of initiative and depressed/anxious mood. In fact, a direct correspondence can be established between the items of the BEL scale and the specific questions asked in SHARE which elicit cognition levels,[19] but given the subjective nature of the answers we felt that the depressive scale EURO-D, also recorded in SHARE, provides a safer option. We adopt the threshold proposed by Dewey and Prince (2005) (having at least 4 disturbances among a set of 12) as a more "objective" indicator of psychological disorders.[20]

In order to be eligible, a patient should score at least 35 on the BEL scale. Eligibility gives access to a monthly cash benefit of €130, irrespective of age, income or need-of-care of the applicant (Table 3.9).

The programme's regulation presents clear similarities with respect to the other two main dependency-assessment tools in Belgium (the BESADL and the APA scale): the evaluation for each task is multi-levelled (from 0 to 3), so that a more precise measure of dependency can be selected for a specific task with respect to those assessments where the evaluation is dichotomous (dependence vs independence); the regulation defines a specific threshold with respect to the evaluation scale, in order to discriminate between those individuals which are on a condition of "objective dependence" (above the threshold) and those who are not (below the threshold)

Table 3.9 Belgian Flanders LTC eligibility rules

Dependency level	*Details*	*Monthly allowance (€)*
Unique	BEL-score of 35 or higher	130

At the same time, the BEL scale presents some specific features: it provides a more detailed characterisation of vulnerability than the APA and the BESADL models; the ADL and iADL are included following the original taxonomy by Katz, Downs, Cash, and Grotz (1970) and Lawton and Brody (1969), while the APA scale does not include all of them—frequently mixing ADL and iADL—and the BESADL scale does not cover iADL limitations at all. Furthermore the BEL scale adds two dimensions of vulnerability, Social ADL and Mental Health, which are neglected in the APA and in the BESADL scales. Including issues on social and mental aspects of frailty seems to bring the BEL scale more into line with the WHO bio-psychosocial perspective (WHO, 2002), and with many geriatric assessments like the "Multi-dimensional geriatric assessment".

3.3 The Czech Republic Příspěvek na péči

Formal programmes of long-term care in the **Czech Republic** offer both in-kind and in-cash benefits. There is no unique institutional body that regulates care services for older people: the health-care sector (the Ministry of Health) mainly covers nursing care at home, while Social Services (the Ministry of Labour and Social Affairs—MoLSA, Ministerstvo práce a sociálních věcí—MPSV) cover other forms of home care and offer dependent individuals a cash allowance.[21] As a consequence, legal rules, eligibility criteria and quality assessment are defined separately by each institution.[22] The Ministry of Labour and Social Affairs refers to long-term care as "a wide range of supportive health and social services provided to people who are no more self-sufficient—either because of their age, disability or for any other serious reason—and thus require constant assistance by another person in coping with their everyday life and daily needs".[23]

Although entitlement for Health-care and Social services in-kind is based on health-care insurance coverage and citizenship, a unique formal definition of "vulnerability" does not exist and the degrees of eligibility depend on individual assessments of need performed either by doctors (for Health-care services) or by social workers (for Social Services). Conversely, the main Czech care allowance for dependent people (*Příspěvek na péči*), firstly introduced with the 2006 Social Services Act,[24] is uniquely regulated throughout the country both for the assessment-of-need process and for the eligibility criteria.

The care allowance is granted to vulnerable individuals more than one year old who are dependent on others for basic tasks of personal care and self-sufficiency, irrespective of their income and age, so that they can "elect the most effective manner of having their needs provided for" (MPSV, 2009). The monetary amount depends on the degree of dependence, and has nature of a care allowance rather than a full reimbursement of the care costs. Vulnerability is defined as an adverse state of health, which is expected to last for at least one year after the first appearance, characterised by limitations in basic life activities like moving, exercise cognitive functioning, communicating, eating, dressing, caring for self-hygiene, using the toilet, performing self-medications, being involved in activities, performing household tasks.

A comprehensive reform of dependency categorisation took place in 2011 when the act of Parliament 366/2011 simplified the evaluation scale and narrowed it down to a list of ten major areas of basic life necessities (each area is mostly a regrouping of the original 36 tasks).[25] Each activity is evaluated on a binary basis (dependent vs independent) (Table 3.10).

Four levels of dependency are distinguished,[26] according to the number of limitations, as Table 3.11 summarises.

To appreciate the magnitude of the benefits, we report as a benchmark the amount of the *basic* pension in the Czech Republic: this is CZK 2550 in 2017, while the *average* pension (single paid out) was CZK 11,441 in 2016.[27]

Applications for the care allowance must be submitted to the regional branches of the MPSV but can be filed on-line through the ministerial portal. The assessment of need follows two steps: a social worker schedules a meeting to assess the degree of vulnerability of the applicant in her "natural environment", while a doctor appointed by the Ministry performs a second evaluation. The final decision on the applicant's eligibility rests with the MPSV regional branch, and can be appealed by the patient. The cash benefit, which is tax-free, can be only spent on care-activities with any provider (Social Services worker, professional caregiver, informal caregiver). Ministerial authorities are in charge of monitoring the proper usage of the cash benefit, and can suspend the allowance in case of misuse.

Table 3.10 Czech Příspěvek na péči assessment of need

Limitation	*Fixed binary value (0/1)*	*SHARE tasks (binary: yes/no)*
Mobility: Walking and transferring	1	Walking across a room *or* Getting in or out of bed
Orientation, ability to hear, see, and use mental functions	1	Disoriented in time (day, week, month, year): Cannot answer three or more
Communicating and understanding	1	Making telephone calls
Cutting up food, eating, drinking, following diet	1	Eating (+ cutting up your food)
Dressing/undressing, putting on shoes	1	Dressing (+ putting on shoes and socks)
Washing the body, combing hair, oral hygiene	1	Bathing or showering
Using toilet, defecating, urinating and cleaning	1	Using the toilet (+ getting up or down)
Self-medications: Following prescribed treatments	1	Taking medications
Engaging in daily routines, age-related activities	1	Preparing a hot meal
Taking care of household, groceries, finances	1	Doing work around the house *or* shopping for groceries *or* managing money

Source: Act No. 366/2011 (§9) amending the Social Services Act 108/2006

Table 3.11 Czech Příspěvek na péči eligibility rules

Dependency level	*Details (old criteria in parenthesis)*	*Monthly allowance*[a]
Light	Dependent in 3–4 activities (12)	€ 33–Kč 880[b]
Medium	Dependent in 5–6 activities (18)	€ 165–Kč 4400
Heavy	Dependent in 7–8 activities (24)	€ 330–Kč 8800
Very heavy	Dependent in 9–10 activities (30)	€ 495–Kč 13,200

Source: Ministerial website, https://portal.mpsv.cz/soc/ssl/prispevek. Currency exchange rate at June 2017

[a]Online source on ministerial website, https://portal.mpsv.cz/soc/ssl/prispevek. Currency exchange rate at June 2017

[b]The allowance for the first dependency level (light) was reduced from Kč 2000 to Kč 800 since 2010. See also Colombo, Llena-Nozal, Mercier, and Tjadens (2011)

A few observations on the Czech assessment criteria are in order. The 2006 version of the assessment-of-need scale was perhaps the most detailed (36 tasks) among those adopted in the major LTC programmes in Europe with the potential exception of the SVaMA [adopted in Italy, see Pilotto et al. (2013)] which nevertheless is built for clinical usage and, in its full version, has no clear threshold to determine dependency. The 2012 version of the scale is simpler, as it consists of ten basic activities which somehow summarise the 36 points of the previous legislation. The ADL limitations are all included in the list, except for the continence item, as well as most of the limitations in iADL.

Dependence in each activity is assessed on a binary yes/no scale, each activity has an equal weight in the computation of the final degree of vulnerability, disregarding possible complementarities: what matters is the overall number of limitations. More specifically, any combination of deficits that reaches the minimum overall count of 3 gives access to the care allowance.

3.4 The French System

3.4.1 Allocation Personnalisée d'Autonomie

There is no single regulation for long-term care policies in **France**. Conversely, a multitude of legislations, actors and sources of financing characterise specific programmes which target various kinds of dependency and vulnerability.[28] A "supplement for assistance of a third party (*majoration pour aide d'une tierce personne*)" and a "supplementary benefit for recourse to a third party" (*prestation complémentaire pour recours à tierce personne*) are offered to non-elderly individuals who already receive an invalidity or a work-injury pension and to those who need help in performing the basic activities of daily life, respectively. The "disability compensation allowance" (*prestation de compensation du handicap*) is instead designed for disabled persons who are younger than 60 years old and who suffer from a degree of disability which meets certain predefined criteria.

With regard to older people, there are three main public sources of long-term care services: (i) the sickness insurance scheme which covers some expenditures for health care; (ii) the retirement insurance scheme, which finances forms of domestic assistance (*Aide sociale aux personnes âgées: aide ménagère à domicile*); and (iii) the Personalised Allowance of Autonomy (APA, A*llocation Personnalisée d'Autonomie*). The latter constitutes the main national programme for tackling dependency among the 60+ population. These LTC programmes target different profiles of vulnerable individuals, yet they adopt a unique evaluation scale to assess their dependency condition: the AGGIR scale.

The **AGGIR** scale (*Autonomie Gérontologique—Groupes Iso-Ressources*) is a national standardised assessment-of-need tool that helps to determine an individual's vulnerability status. The scale, introduced in 1997 and modified in 2001, 2004 and 2008,[29] evaluates limitations in ADL and iADL and generates an index measure from 1 to 6 that represents a patient's vulnerability classification. Each category, or Group Iso-Resources (GIR), gathers individuals with a similar loss of autonomy and equivalent need-of-care. GIR 1 represents the hardship case (0 per cent of autonomy), while GIR 6 corresponds to the non-vulnerable level (93 per cent of autonomy, or higher).[30]

The AGGIR assessment is a compound of two groups of variables: (i) Ten "discriminatory" variables, eight of which are actually contributing to a determination of the final vulnerability score (six variables related to physical limitations and difficulties in ADL, two variables on psychical deficits—coherence and orientation; (ii) two variables related to iADL (outdoor movement, distant communication), which do not contribute to determine the AGGIR score.

Seven "illustrative" variables, mainly related to limitations in iADL tasks, provide a measure of contextual factors and are used to evaluate how much assistance a person needs to lead a normal social life, while not entering directly the algorithm of the AGGIR score.[31]

Each variable (item) in the French AGGIR scale is evaluated on a three-step scale (A, B, C or 1, 2, 3), depending on the degree of limitation experienced by the patient in the specific task.[32] For the usual issue that in SHARE we do not have information on the intensity of the reported limitations, we assign the label B (the intermediate level) whenever a respondent reports a limitation in a specific task (Table 3.12).

The illustrative variables (each to be evaluated on the A, B, C scale), are: managing money, preparing meals, performing housekeeping tasks, using transportation modes while outdoor, shopping, follow medical prescriptions, doing leisure activities.

Through the use of a rather complex algorithm,[33] AGGIR splits the population into six iso-groups[34] depending on how they perform in the first eight discriminatory tasks.[35] Belonging to one group rather than

Table 3.12 France's AGGIR assessment of need

Discriminatory variables	*Description*	*Assigned value*	*SHARE tasks*
Coherence	Converse or behave in a logical and sensible manner	2 out of 3	Disoriented in time (day, week, month, year): Cannot answer three or more
Orientation	Locates oneself in time and space		
Toileting	Upper and lower body hygiene	2 out of 3	Bathing or showering
Dressing	Upper, middle and lower body dressing	2 out of 3	Dressing (+ putting on shoes and socks)
Alimentation	Serving and eating	2 out of 3	Eating (+cutting up your food)
Elimination	Using the toilet for urine/faecal eliminations	2 out of 3	Using the toilet (+ getting up or down)
Transfers	Lying down, sitting down, getting up	2 out of 3	Getting in or out of bed
Indoor movement	With or without technical assistance	2 out of 3	Walking across a room
Outdoor movement	Same as above, but outdoors	2 out of 3	Walking across a room *or* using a map to figure out how to get around in a strange place
Distant communication	Using the phone and tele-alarm	2 out of 3	Making telephone calls

Source: Adapted from Dupourqué, Schoonveld, and Bushey (2012)

another will determine which LTC benefit an individual can claim for (if any). Table 3.13 briefly outlines the six vulnerability categories.

From the previous table it is clear that the mental and physical limitations play almost independent roles in defining a vulnerability condition. Regardless of the other functional deficits in ADL, those who have mental limitations are assigned to, at least, GIR 2. Conversely, those with difficulties in—roughly—at least two ADL are categorised in GIR 4 regardless of their mental health. This combination holds whenever the limitations are reported with at least a B intensity score. It should be noted that being limited in "moving inside the house" is not a sufficient limitation for GIR 4 if the only other loss of autonomy concerns the "transferring" task. In order to determine GIR 4, when the "mobility" limitation is selected, at

Table 3.13 France AGGIR vulnerability categorisation

GIR group	*Description*
GIR 1	Bedridden or confined to an armchair, with seriously impaired mental functions
GIR 2	Those confined to bed, needing assistance for most ADL (typically toileting, dressing, elimination, alimentation), with mental functions not entirely compromised. Those with severe mental deficits but with no serious limitations in mobility and personal care functions.
GIR 3	Those with no serious mental and mobility limitations, who need help several times a day for ADL (typically for hygiene and elimination tasks) while not requiring constant monitoring.
GIR 4	Those who have transferring limitation, but once up can move around indoors. They sometimes need help with bathing and dressing, and most of them can eat without assistance. Alternatively, those with no mobility or transferring limitations, but who need help to perform other ADL, including eating.
GIR 5	Those who can move around inside their home without assistance, and can eat and dress themselves alone. They require occasional help with bathing, preparing meals and doing housework.
GIR 6	Those who have not lost their autonomy for daily living activities.

Source: Dupourqué et al. (2012)

least one more limitation should be selected among the following: "using the toilet", "dressing", "eating" or "bathing". Finally, as stated before, limitations in iADL do not play a role in defining the GIR score.

The outcome of the AGGIR evaluation defines eligibility for the APA programme in France, but it is also included in the eligibility rules for the Social Assistance to seniors (see below).

The **APA**[36] (*Allocation Personnalisée d'Autonomie*, Personalised Allowance of Autonomy) has been introduced in 2001, in place of the previous LTC programme "*Prestation Spécifique Dépendance*" (PSD). It is managed at the *départmental* level[37] and provides to vulnerable older individuals residing in France an in-kind benefit whose intent is to finance a personalised assistance scheme, for both institutional care and home care. The level of the benefit varies according to the recipient's health status and the level of disposable income, although means-testing plays no role in initially defining eligibility. It should be noted that the rules are slightly different between the APA for home-care beneficiaries

Table 3.14 French APA eligibility rules

APA eligibility criteria	*Description*
Residency	Being resident in France
Age	At least 60 years old
Vulnerability	At least GIR4

and for nursing-care residents, given the focus of this book we will discuss home-based LTC. The APA "à domicile" represents the implementation of a plan of long-term assistance, personalised according to individual need. Three entry conditions are necessary in order for the allowance to be granted: (i) the applicant must be resident in France; (ii) they must be at least 60 years old; and (iii) they must exhibit a vulnerability level of at least GIR 4. Table 3.14 summarises these three criteria.

The assessment is performed by medical professionals, paramedicals or social workers, usually at the applicant's place, after a proper application has been submitted to the local Social Community Centre. If the assessed vulnerability ISO group is at least GIR 4, the evaluators develop a personalised care scheme, which comprises all the tasks that should be performed in order to help the beneficiary to live a comfortable life in his/her own home. Such tasks include nursing home care, meals on wheels, social assistance, housework, technical assistance with aids. The APA is designed to (partially) finance this care plan, with no time limitations. The maximum monthly APA contributions are summarised in Table 3.15, by GIR group.

The actual monetary amount, and therefore the extent to which APA will contribute to the care plan, depends not only on the GIR classification but also on the applicant's income (together with the partner's income if in a couple). If an applicant's monthly income lies below €800.53, the whole of the care plan is financed by the APA. For higher incomes, the individual's contribution to the care plan increases linearly from 0 per cent up to a ceiling of 90 per cent of the total cost, which is paid by those who have a monthly income equal or higher than €2948.16. Having ascertained the patient's costs share, the APA benefit is determined as the difference between the total care-plan amount and the patient contribution.

The allowance is usually paid directly to the professional caregivers, or to the care receiver who must then provide proofs of expenditures. APA can be suspended if this documentation is not provided, or if random audits and controls confirm abuse of the allowance.

Table 3.15 French APA benefits' amount

GIR group	*Maximum APA allowance (monthly amount in euro)*
GIR 1	1714.79
GIR 2	1376.91
GIR 3	994.87
GIR 4	663.61
GIR 5	Non-eligible
GIR 6	Non-eligible

Source: Governmental source: https://www.service-public.fr/particuliers/vosdroits/F1802. Monetary amounts at 01/01/2017

3.4.2 *Aide ménagère à domicile*

While APA is designed to target vulnerability profiles with numerous limitations in ADL, the **Social Assistance to seniors** (***Aide sociale aux personnes âgées***) is an in-kind benefit aimed at providing home-help (*Aide ménagère à domicile*) to older people who report lower degrees of dependency and are therefore not necessarily eligible for the APA allowance.[38] The programme is intended to support older people with cooking, washing and bathing, shopping for groceries and for the small and common tasks of daily living. It also provides moral support to individuals living alone, involving them in conversations.

In order to be eligible to the Social Assistance to seniors, three conditions must be met by the applicant, as Table 3.16 highlights: a minimum age requirement of 65 years old; the presence of limitations in daily activities related to personal hygiene and to small acts of daily livings (e.g., laundry- and home-care, meals preparation and shopping for groceries) classifiable as GIR 5 or GIR 6; not being a beneficiary of the APA nor eligible to it; having a monthly income up to €801 for singles or €1243 for couples. It cannot be combined with APA. The programme is not means-tested but, as with APA, the amount of service costs covered by the *Action Sociale* will depend on applicants' resources. In order to simulate eligibility for *Aide Sociale*, we exploit the following SHARE information: "Bathing or showering", "Preparing a hot meal" and "shopping for groceries". In order to perform a prudent implementation of the regulation, we exclude the SHARE task "doing work around the house or garden", as it seems overly generic with respect to the *Aide ménagère rationale*.

Table 3.16 French *Aide ménagère à domicile* eligibility rules

Aide ménagère eligibility criteria	*Description*	*SHARE information*
Age	At least 65 years old	Age
Vulnerability	Needing assistance with personal hygiene/meals preparation/ shopping for groceries	Bathing or showing/preparing a hot meal/shopping for groceries
Non-cumulation	Not receiving APA allowance	Eligibility for APA (see previous paragraph)
Monthly income	Less than €801 (single) or €1243 (couple)	

As detailed in the previous paragraphs, GIR5 is a level of vulnerability which does not grant eligibility to the APA programme.[39] It principally includes individuals with limitations in doing housework and iADL, or those with difficulties in the areas of washing or bathing. This eligibility rule stresses the complementary nature of the *Aide Sociale* programme, which is able to offer a minimum coverage to older people who still face difficulties in everyday activities, but to a lower extent with respect to the APA recipients. Limitations in the instrumental activities of daily livings (iADL) like those included in GIR5 or GIR6 are known to be the first signals of an ongoing process of vulnerability. While they cannot trigger eligibility to the APA on their own, they are the main target of the *Aide Sociale* programme.

Depending on applicants' resources, the home-care services will be financed by the *départment* (through Social Assistance) or by the applicants' retirement insurance (a major example is the *Caisse Nationale d'Assurance Vieillesse*—CNAV). With reard to the year 2014, the *départment*'s intervention is limited to those cases in which the applicant's monthly income is lower than €791.99 (€1229.61 if he/she lives with a partner). For those earning more than €791.99 per month, the retirement insurances will finance a share of the total expenditure needed for the home-care services, depending on the applicant's income level. To make few examples, those living alone with an income lower than €1140 will not contribute more than 36 per cent of overall costs, while they will pay 73 per cent when earning more than €1423. Those living in a couple will contribute just 10 per cent when they have an income lower than €1451, while their contribution will be at its highest (73 per cent) after they exceed the earning threshold of €2134.[40]

3.5 The German *Pflegeversicherung*

The **German** long-term care system was established by the 1994 Long-term Care Act which became effective in 1995 (the Law on social protection for the Long-term-care risk, *Gesetz zur sozialen Absicherung des Risikos der Pflegebedürftigkeit*), introducing a mandatory Long-term care Insurance[41] (*Pflegeversicherung*) for German citizens as an additional pillar of the national Welfare State.[42] The long-term care insurance specifically targets vulnerable individuals who suffer from physical or mental limitations that prevent them from performing basic and regular tasks of daily living.[43] It provides them with benefits in cash and/or in kind, in order to ease the costs of home care assistance. From a financial point of view, the LTC insurance is not a full insurance, since it still requires the individuals to contribute to the care expenditure, depending on their level of vulnerability. In addition, other services such as nursing courses for caregivers or nursing aids are provided. It is also worth noting that home care, alongside with policies of prevention and rehabilitation, is stressed in the law (SGB XI, §3, §5) as a crucial component of the Long-term care in Germany: its major goal is to keep the vulnerable individual in his/her own home environment, delaying institutionalisation and in-patient care.[44]

There are four main forms of LTC benefits that are available to an eligible insured individual: (i) cash benefits for home care (*Pflegegeld*); (ii) benefits in kind for home care (*Pflegesachleistung*); (iii) day and night home care (*Tagespflege und Nachtpflege*); (iv) institutional care in nursing homes (*Vollstationäre Pflege*).[45] Among home-care services, individuals can choose between an exclusive cash benefit, an exclusive domestic-care programme in kind or a combination of the two (*Kombinationsleistung*).[46] Cash benefits are paid directly from the insurance fund to the dependent person who can use them at his/her discretion to compensate a self-procured caregiver; the benefits are not treated as income and thus are tax-free. Benefits in kind (community care) consist in personal-care and domestic-help service provided by professional carers, usually a licensed home care service. Professional help is considerably more expensive than private aid; therefore, the budget of in-kind benefits is higher than for the cash programmes (Table 3.19). It is important to note that the LTCI funds will contribute to the expenditures up to a maximum amount (SGB XI §§36–45; see also Table 3.19). Should the total cost of care exceed this amount, the remaining part will be paid directly by the beneficiary or a social welfare office. Conversely, when the in-kind allowance is not fully utilised, the applicant can claim for a partial in-cash benefit for the remaining share, thus realising the *Kombinationsleistung* scheme Rothgang (2010).

In all cases, eligibility depends on the level of vulnerability of the insured person (need of assistance, *Hilfebedürftigkeit*), while other characteristics, such as economic resources, age or availability of informal caregivers, are not taken into account. Vulnerability is assessed by the medical service of the health insurance companies. The assessment focuses on those limitations which are likely to last in the long term, i.e., for a minimum of six months, because of a physical or mental illness or disability. Since a major reform of both assessment and eligibility rules came into practice since 2017, we will describe both the pre-2017 and post-2017 legislations.

3.5.1 Regulation Before 2017

The medical evaluation covers four main areas of daily activities: personal care, nutrition, moving—which constitute *basis care activities* and mainly refer to ADL tasks—and household activities, which resemble iADL tasks. The old version of §14 in SGB XI lists the main areas of activities that should be evaluated to assess the patient's vulnerability, with their respective tasks. In the case of each task the nurses and/or the physicians should evaluate the amount of care that would take to a non-professional caregiver to provide assistance, in terms of minutes per task. To ensure the same standards for all patients, nationwide guidelines were specified for most tasks. The time measures, reported in Table 3.17, refer to a single task occurrence and serve as a guideline to the operator in order to calculate the daily demand for care.

Similar to the Austrian system, the German vulnerability assessment is particularly detailed with respect to tasks of personal care: even small activities such as combing, shaving or dental care are assigned a specific guideline amount of time, and specific attention is paid to those individuals who have to deal with urinary drainage or ostomy bags. Furthermore, tasks regarding nutrition are divided into a preparatory phase (preparing bite-sized food) and an eating phase; the movement-related activities are also analytically separated, even though only a few of them have specific time-requirement guidelines while the remaining must be evaluated on an individual basis. Household activities are characterised by several tasks, though time requirements are not specified a priori. It is worth noting that two of the limitations in iADL (managing money and communication—using the

Table 3.17 German *Pflegeversicherung* assessment of need, pre-2017

Basic care	*Limitations*	*Need-of-care (minutes per task)*	*Assumed daily need in SHARE*	*SHARE tasks (binary: yes/no)*
✓	Washing body (upper- lower- body, hands)	20–25	40′	Bathing or showering
✓	Dental care	5	10′	Bathing or showering
✓	Combing	1–3	–	Bathing or showering
✓	Shaving	5–10	–	Bathing or showering
✓	Taking a shower	15–20	6′	Bathing or showering
✓	Bathing	20–25		
✓	Defecation and urination	8	32′	Using the toilet
	If also dependent for: Mobility inside the house, add	2	8′	(+getting up or down)
✓	Maintenance of urinary drainage bag/ostomy bag	2–4 each	–	–
✓	Incontinence	11	44′	Incontinence or involuntary loss of urine
✓	Bite-sized food preparation	2–3	51′	Eating (+cutting up your food)
✓	Food in-take	15–20		
✓	Moving in and out of bed/changing positions	1–3 each	4′	Getting in or out of bed
✓	Dressing-undressing (upper- lower body)	Unspecified	12′	Dressing (+ putting on shoes and socks)
✓	Moving inside house	Unspecified	30′[a]	Walking across a room
✓	Standing (transferring)	Unspecified	–	Getting in or out of bed
✓	Climbing stairs	Unspecified	–	Climbing one flight of stairs without resting
✓	Leaving and returning to house	Unspecified	20′[a]	Walking across a room
×	Shopping	Unspecified	20′[a]	Shopping for groceries
×	Cooking	Unspecified	60’	Preparing a hot meal
×	Cleaning dwelling	Unspecified	60′[a]	Doing work around the house
×	Washing dishes,	Unspecified		
×	Washing and ironing clothes,	Unspecified		
×	Managing the heating	Unspecified		

[a]Guidelines in brackets are taken from the Austrian legislation (Table 3.1)

telephone) are excluded from the list. An important difference with the Austrian framework relies on the role of the time requirements guidelines, which are defined *per task* rather than *per day*. This allows for a greater flexibility in designing a personalised programme of care: for instance, even though the time requirements for bathing are fixed at 20–25 minutes, not every person takes a daily bath. The amount of time for bathing could therefore be just a fraction of the bathing occurrences during a week: if an individual takes a bath twice a week, he/she will require 40 minutes of care every seven days, equating to a daily requirement of around six minutes. As a further example, this flexibility (and the lower degree of standardisation between individuals) will also apply to the number of daily occurrences of defecation/urination and nutrition.

Some doubts have been cast on the peculiarity of this assessment tool, which focuses principally on physical limitation and takes insufficient account of the specific needs of people with mental deficits. Rothgang (2010) highlighted that such a "tight definition of dependency meant that people with dementia are entitled to LTCI benefits only insofar as they need help with the activities of daily living, as the assessment did not evaluate or take into account their general need for supervision". This shortfall has been partially addressed through the provisions of the 2012 reform, which have resulted in more attention being devoted to those individuals who are limited in their daily activities because of mental illnesses and cognitive limitations. These individuals, regarded as "at risk of being a danger to themselves or to others", were included in the taxonomy of vulnerability under the label PEA (*Personen mit eingeschränkter Alltagskompetenz*, People impaired in activities of daily living).[47]

The German legislation did not entail fixed time guidelines for the iADL limitations (which mostly correspond to the so-called "non-basic activities" in the scale): indeed, in Table 3.17, some limitations have an "unspecified" time requirement in the "need-of-care" column. The term "unspecified" was referring to the fact that the amount of care should be evaluated on an individual basis by the assessment team. When we match these rules with the actual limitations observed in the SHARE data for the German case, we exploit the strong similarities existing between the German and the Austrian assessments of need. They are both highly detailed in terms of assigning to each task a measure of need-of-care expressed in units of time. We therefore impute the limitations having "unspecified" requirements with the corresponding time guidelines coming from the Austrian *Pflegegeld* system (moving inside the house, leaving

Table 3.18 German *Pflegeversicherung* eligibility rules

	Assistance for basic care (personal care, feeding, mobility)	*Assistance for household activities*	*Minimum requirements of care-needs per day*
Level 1	At least once a day for at least 2 tasks from one or more areas	Several times a week	Overall: 90′ (45′ for basic care)
Level 2	At least thrice a day for at least 2 tasks from one or more areas	Several times a week	Overall: 180′ (120′ for basic care)
Level 3	Help needed around the clock	Several times a week	Overall: 300′ (240′ for basic care)
Hardship level	Those in level 3 who need assistance for at least 420 min a day with at least 120 min during the night, or who need simultaneous help from multiple caregivers		
Cognitive impairment	Following the 2012 reform, individuals affected by cognitive impairment are given access to an additional allowance, irrespective of their functional disability status (even if they are classified as Level 0 (*Pflegestufe 0*).		

and returning to the house, shopping, cooking, and doing housework). To take just one example, the "cooking" task has a time requirement of 30 hours/month (1 hour per day) in Austria, which translates into 60 minutes per day in Germany.[48]

As a result of the evaluation process, each patient is then categorised according to three levels of need (Pflegestufen I, II, III; see Table 3.18), defined by the original legislation, which differ with respect to the number of limitations, the estimated amount of care time requested, and the balance between limitations in ADL and iADL.

In order to meet eligibility for care, an individual must exhibit a minimum requirements of daily care-needs are an overall need for 90 minutes of help, with at least 45 minutes attributable to basic care tasks (level 1; *Pflegestufe I*). The 2012 reform introduced new rules to account in full for mental illness.[49] For the same level of vulnerability, being affected by cognitive/mental limitations (PEA) gives access to an additional allowance; furthermore, those patients who do not qualify for level-1 benefits (patients with "level 0"/"Pflegestufe 0") can still receive an allowance if they suffer from mental disorders. Table 3.19 provides details about how the vulnerability levels relate to the amount of LTC benefit for which an insured individual is entitled to claim. The monetary amounts reflect the

Table 3.19 German *Pflegeversicherung* benefits' amount (valid before January 2017)

Level	*Home care*		*Day & Night*	*Nursing home care*
	€ in-cash §37	*€ in-kind §36*	*€ in-kind §41*	*€ in-kind §43*
Level 0 (PEA)	123	231		
Level 1	244	468	468	1064
Level 1 (PEA)	305 from 1/2012 316 from 1/2015	665 from 1/2012 689 from 1/2015		
Level 2	440 from 1/2012 458 from 1/2015	1100 from 1/2012 1444 from 1/2015	1100 from 1/2012 1144 from 1/2015	1279 1330 from 1/2015
Level 2 (PEA)	525 from 1/2012 545 from 1/2015	1250 from 1/2012 1298 from 1/2015		
Level 3	700 from 1/2012 728 from 1/2015	1550 from 1/2012 1612 from 1/2015	1550 from 1/2012 1612 from 1/2015	1550 from 1/2012 1612 from 1/2015

PEA (Personen mit eingeschränkter Alltagskompetenz, Individuals impaired in activities of daily living) are individuals with limited or compromised cognitive ability

latest reform (June 2014).[50] For those who do not suffer from mental illnesses, level 1 is the minimum vulnerability level that entitles them to access LTC services.

3.5.2 *The System Post-2017*

Since 2017, following the recent reform (Bäcker, 2016; BMG, 2015; Kalwitzki et al., 2015), the process of assessing individuals' vulnerability is developed according to six modules: Mobility; Cognitive abilities (mostly related to orientation, understanding and memory); Behavioural and mental problems; Limitations in ADL; Coping with illness and therapy; and Social participation. Two additional modules, "performing activities outside the house" and "limitations in iADL", are assessed but do not contribute to the overall score nor to the eligibility decision, conversely to the pre-reform rules.

Each module includes several outcomes which are valued on a scale taking any integer value between 0 and 3, with higher numbers meaning a higher level of dependency.[51] Table 3.20 summarises the outcomes included in the assessment, together with the link we performed in the SHARE data. As usual, since in SHARE we lack information on the intensity of the limitations reported by the respondent, we assign the "most common dependency level" (e.g., 2 out of 3) when the respondent reports a limitation in a specific task.

Within the Mobility module, a close correspondence can be established. The Cognitive module involves several outcomes regarding orientation or understanding ability; since an outcome-specific link could be established only in the case of some SHARE items, we chose to evaluate this module as a whole by using the "orientation" index (not being able to answer three or more questions on time—day, week, month, year) and the "recall" variable (recalling less than three words out of ten). We aim, therefore, to reduce the effect of self-report bias and inaccuracy potentially embedded in specific respondents' answers, and to effectively identify serious cognitive conditions through the most 'objective' outcomes (orientation and recall) adopted by the literature in this field (Castro-Costa et al., 2007). A similar approach is followed for the Psychological section, where, as explained for the Belgian Flanders scheme, given the potential inherent subjective interpretation of the single SHARE questions on the topic, we adopt the widely adopted EURO-D threshold of 4 points (or higher) as a more accurate predictor of latent psychological issues. The fourth module largely resembles the ADL items covered in SHARE, with the exception of "drinking" and "faecal incontinence", which cannot be matched. The fifth module is primarily concerned with assessing whether the individual can cope independently with simple or elaborate illness-related requirements (e.g., taking medications, insulin injections, therapeutic activity, stoma-care routine). Each outcome is evaluated in terms of the frequency of assistance required by the applicant (daily, weekly, monthly). Since SHARE only covers the "taking medication" outcome, and no information can be retrieved on the frequency of assistance needed, this module cannot be matched with the micro-data. Finally, in the module on Everyday Life we are able to match three outcomes out of six.

Within each module, the sum of outcomes is computed and then converted in an eligibility score, following the guidelines and grids summarised in Table 3.21.

Table 3.20 German *Pflegeversicherung* and SHARE, since 2017

Limitation	*Assigned value*	*SHARE tasks (binary: yes/no)*
1. Mobility		
Change of position in bed	2 out of 3	Getting in or out of bed
Hold the stable seating position	2 out of 3	Sitting for about 2 h
Standing up/sitting down	2 out of 3	Getting up from a chair after sitting for long periods
Move within the living area	2 out of 3	Walking across a room
Stair climbing	2 out of 3	Climbing one flight of stairs without resting
2. Cognitive and communicative skills (Identify people from the surrounding area; Local orientation; Time orientation; Memory; Perform multi-step daily operations; Making decisions in everyday life; Understanding facts and information; Identify risks and hazards; Communication of elementary needs; Understanding of Prompts; Participation in a conversation)	Valued as a whole in the vulnerability scale	Disoriented in time (day, week, month, year): cannot answer three or more Recall: less than 30% words
3. Behavioural and psychological problems (Motorised behavioural problems; Nocturnal restlessness; Self-injurious and auto aggressive behaviour; Damage to objects; Physically aggressive behaviour towards other people; Verbal aggression; Other vocal abnormalities; Defence or other supportive measures; Delusions, misunderstandings; fears; Impotence, depressive mood; Social inadequate behaviour; Other inadequate actions)	Valued as a whole in the vulnerability scale	*EURO-D score 4+*
4. Dependency in ADL		
Wash the front upper body	2 out of 3	Bathing or showering
Combing, dental care/prosthesis cleaning, shaving	–	Bathing or showering
Wash the intimate area	2 out of 3	Bathing or showering
Showers or bathing	2 out of 3	Bathing or showering
Fitting and lining the upper & lower body	4 out of 6	Dressing (+ putting on shoes and socks)
Cutting-up the food, pouring beverages	2 out of 3	Eating (+ cutting up your food)

(*continued*)

Table 3.20 (continued)

Limitation	*Assigned value*	*SHARE tasks (binary: yes/no)*
Eating	6 out of 9	Eating (+ cutting up your food)
Drinking	–	–
Use the toilet/toilet-chair	4 out of 6	Using the toilet (+ getting up or down)
Consequences of urinary incontinence, dealing with permanent catheter/urostoma	2 out of 3	Incontinence or involuntary loss of urine
Consequences of a faecal incontinence, dealing with stoma	–	–
5. Dealing with illness and therapy-related requirements and stress		–
6. Designing everyday life and social contacts		
In control for planning routines and activities	–	–
Resting and sleeping	2 out of 3	Having had trouble sleeping recently
To keep oneself busy performing enjoyable activities	2 out of 3	"What have you enjoyed doing recently"—Fails to mention any enjoyable activity
Plan for the future (longer periods of time, make weekly or monthly schedule)	–	–
Interaction with people in direct contact	–	–
Contact management to persons outside the direct environment	2 out of 3	No activity performed in the last month OR Unable to use the telephone
Not considered for eligibility		
7. Out-of-home activities (iADL tasks)		
8. Household management (shopping for daily needs; preparation of simple meals; easy (clean) cleaning and cleaning; elaborate (heavy) clearing and cleaning; use of services; settlement of financial matters; regulation of administrative matters)		

Source: SGB XI (Buch des Sozialgesetzbuches), §14

The sum of all the eligibility scores, which ranges from 0 to 100, represents the individual's vulnerability score, which is then used to determine access to benefits. In particular, whereas the pre-reform regulation classified individuals in four categories, corresponding to increasing levels of

Table 3.21 German *Pflegeversicherung* correspondence grid for eligibility score

	Level of dependency				
	0	*1*	*2*	*3*	*4*
	None	*Low*	*Considerable*	*Severe*	*Hardest*
Module					
1 *Mobility (sum of outcomes values)*	0–1	2–3	4–5	6–9	10–15
Module 1 eligibility score	**0**	**2.5**	**5**	**7.5**	**10**
2 Cognitive *(sum of outcomes values)*	0–1	2–5	6–10	11–16	17–33
Matching with SHARE variables				Disoriented in time	Disoriented in time & recall less than 30%
3 Depression *(sum of outcomes values)*	0	1–2	3–4	5–6	7–65
Matching with SHARE variables				Euro-D ≥ 4	
Modules 2, 3 eligibility score (the highest is considered)	**0**	**3.75**	**7.5**	**11.25**	**15**
4 Dependency in ADL *(sum of outcomes values)*	0–2	3–7	8–18	19–36	37–54
Module 4 eligibility score	**0**	**10**	**20**	**30**	**40**
5 *Therapy-related requirements*	–	–	–	–	–
Module 5 eligibility score	**0**	**5**	**10**	**15**	**20**
6 *Everyday life (sum of outcomes values)*	0	1–3	4–6	7–11	12–18
Module 6 eligibility score	**0**	**3.75**	**7.5**	**11.256**	**15**

Source: SGB XI (Buch des Sozialgesetzbuches), §14

need (0, I, II, III), the current rules introduce a five-step categorisation as detailed. The minimum score granting access to the in-cash or in-kind benefits is 27, which corresponds to Grade of care II or *Pflegegrad 2* (up to the score of 47.5). Table 3.22 summarises the benefits' values granted to each care-need level.

Table 3.22 German *Pflegeversicherung* benefits' amount (valid from January 2017)

Level (Pflegegrad)	*Home care*		*Residential care*
	€ in-cash	*€ in-kind*	*€ in-kind*
PG 1			125
PG 2	316	689	770
PG 3	545	1298	1262
PG 4	728	1612	1775
PG 5	901	1995	2005

Source: Ministry of Health, http://www.pflegestaerkungsgesetz.de/finanzielle-leistungen/pflegegeld-fuer-haeusliche-pflege/

3.6 The Italian LTC Programmes

The Italian LTC programmes operate mostly at the regional level and the lack of harmonisation has produced a patchwork of schemes, which differ in terms of the benefits and services provided, and also in terms of the target population and eligibility rules. In order to provide a comprehensive taxonomy of the Italian case, we think it is useful to start from a national provision *Indennità di Accompagnamento*, which—strictly speaking—does not belong to the LTC domain. We will then proceed to describe the main regional LTC programmes.[52]

A nationwide cash benefit, the *Indennità di Accompagnamento* (IA), is available to Italian individuals classified as *invalid*, although the definition of invalidity itself is rather broad and inclusive: blind individuals, physically or mentally disabled individuals (100 per cent disability), individuals in need of constant assistance for walking or performing activities of daily living. There are no explicit guidelines for the assessment and evaluation of such outcomes: in practice, applications for IA benefit are made through the National Social Insurance Agency, conditional to the existence of a certificate of invalidity issued by a General Practitioner. The IA corresponds to a monthly cash benefit of €512.34.[53]

Also operating at the national level is "National Fund for the Loss of Autonomy" (FNNA, *Fondo Nazionale Non Autosufficienza*) established with the intent to provide basic assistance to individuals suffering from a loss of autonomy.[54] The resources are allocated to regions, which administer specific programmes of care, either in-kind or in-cash, with a principal focus on domiciliary care (residential care programmes are also implemented, however). Moreover, several regions chose to complement the national resources with a Regional Fund for the loss of autonomy (FRNA, *Fondo Regionale per la Non Autosufficienza*): specifically, a FRNA has been established in Bolzano,[55] Friuli-Venezia Giulia, Liguria, Veneto, Emilia-Romagna, Marche, Umbria, Lazio, Toscana, Puglia, Basilicata, Calabria and Sardegna. The regional programmes, financed through either FNNA or FRNA, are split according to the targeted population. Namely, the legislations differentiate between individuals with an "extremely severe disability" (*disabilità gravissima*) or a "severe disability" (*disabilità grave*). The former category implies a loss of autonomy, whose clinical profiles are thoroughly described in the legislation,[56] while the identification of a "severe disability" is left to the assessment of each regional authority.[57]

The level of vulnerability corresponding to "extremely severe disability" and the related loss of autonomy corresponds to a situation which would almost surely grant eligibility for domiciliary care in the other European countries. But these are not the cases which are of interest to us, as in the other European countries older people qualify for LTC for conditions which entail a milder loss of autonomy. Hence, we turn the attention to the case of "severe disability".

In the follow sections, we present a review of the regional programmes (funded either through the FNNA or the FRNA) targeting conditions of "severe disability" and loss of autonomy at a regional level, showing the wide variability of approaches prevailing in Italy. We will present all the available information in the Tables 3.23 up to Table 3.40 as well as in the Appendix A.2, however we will discuss in detail only a few cases—namely, the schemes implemented in Bolzano, Campania, Toscana and Veneto.

3.6.1 The Italian Regional Programmes

As we argued in the previous section, the wide regional variability in LTC provisions and eligibility rules prevailing in Italy would require an extensive survey, which is beyond the scope of this book. In order to describe the distinguishing features of the regional programmes, we present some representative cases.

At one extreme we find the LTC scheme operating in the **province of Bolzano**, which provides LTC as well as some partial coverage of the costs faced by caregivers within the household, but also cash benefits to cover costs for residential homes.[58] Individuals who need at least two hours per day of care (on average) for a period of six months or more, can apply for

Table 3.23 The Bolzano province's VITA scale for assessing needs

Limitation	*Min-max reference minutes/die*	*Assigned minutes/die*	*SHARE tasks*
Nutrition			
Taking main meals (including cutting up the food)	10–90	74	Eating (+cutting up your food)
Taking light meals and liquids	10–60	50	Eating (+cutting up your food)
Enteral nutrition	30–180	–	–
Taking medications	1–15	12.2	Taking medications
Personal hygiene			
Washing body and bathing	5–30	25	Bathing or showering
Washing intimate areas	5–15	13	Bathing or showering
Oral hygiene	3–18	15	Bathing or showering
Combing	1–6	–	–
Face care	2–10	8.4	Bathing or showering
Other minor care (massages, nails, lotions)	2–10	–	–
Prophylaxis for pneumonia and thrombosis	2–20	–	–
Vital signs monitoring	2–30	–	–
Toilet needs			
Help for urinating or defecating	4–40	32.8	Using the toilet (+ getting up or down)
Help with tampons	2–20	–	–
Additional help for those with urinary or faecal incontinence	5–20	17	Incontinence or involuntary loss of urine
Maintenance of catheters/ stoma	5–20	–	–
Help for mobility-related issues			
Getting in and out of bed	2–12	10	Getting in or out of bed
Help for dressing and undressing	3–20	16.6	Dressing (+ putting on shoes and socks)
Moving around to deal with activities	2–50	40.4	Walking across a room
Transferring	2–20	16.4	Getting in or out of bed
Placement in bed	2–40	32.4	Getting in or out of bed
Moving outside the house (leaving and getting back to the house)	10–60	50	Walking across a room
Exercising	2–30	–	

(*continued*)

Table 3.23 (continued)

Limitation	*Min-max reference minutes/die*	*Assigned minutes/die*	*SHARE tasks*
Psychosocial needs			
Need for surveillance and/or intervention	10–180	146	Disoriented in time (day, week, month, year): Cannot answer three or more
Keeping social relationships	10–60	50	EURO-D score 4+
Help with organising daily activities	10–60	–	–
Domestic activities			
Shopping for groceries	–	20[a]	Shopping for groceries
Cooking and prepare meals	–	60[a]	Preparing a hot meal
Cleaning the house and doing house-tasks	–	20[a]	Doing work around the house
Washing underwear and towels	–	20[a]	Doing work around the house
Heating the dwelling	–	20[a]	Doing work around the house
Other activities	–	–	–

Source: Provincial resolution, 28 January 2014, no. 73

[a]Guidelines in brackets are borrowed from the Austrian legislation (Table 3.1). Domestic activities account for a maximum of 30 (15) minutes per day if the overall need for the remaining areas exceeds 142 (105) minutes per day

LTC. The evaluation process is based on the assessment of needs for limitations in ADL and is measured in units of time of care,[59] it adopts a scale known as *VITA*,[60] which takes into account five *basic care needs* (from the ADL) and a set of iADL limitations as detailed in Table 3.23. The latter are included only if an individual exhibits a daily average basic care need of more than 105 care minutes. The weights attached to the iADL limitations is somewhat residual: for applicants with a daily care amount higher than 142 minutes, the maximum care load from the instrumental activities is 30 minutes per day, while a basic care need between 105 and 141 minutes per day, the amount of care granted for the instrumental activities up to 15 minutes per day. For levels of basic care lower than 105 minutes per day, iADL needs are not included in the assessment.

Since SHARE does not allow to measure the intensity of a loss of autonomy, we decided to assign 80 per cent of the maximum potential amount of care attached to each limitation, as for the iADL, the VITA

Table 3.24 Bolzano's vulnerability and eligibility levels for Assegno di Cura (year 2017)

Level	*Need-of-care in minutes/die*	*Cash benefit in Euro*
0	0–119	0 (not eligible)
1	120–239	558.5
2	240–359	900
3	360–479	1350
4	480+	1800

Source: Updated according to official website at http://www.retecivica.bz.it/it/servizi/servizi-categorie.asp?bnsvf_svid=1009600

scale does not fix time guidelines, hence we exploited the strong similarities existing between the programme operating in Bolzano and the Austrian assessments of need and attach the corresponding amount of care to each iADL limitation.

As a result of the overall need-of-care assessment, individuals are assigned to five vulnerability levels, which are outlined in Table 3.24.

The legislation defines as eligible for care all those with a minimum need for care of 120 minutes per day (Level 1). Eligibility is not means-tested and age-independent. However, there is a requirement of a minimum 15 years of residence within the province of Bolzano or a continuous residence for the last 5 years before the one in which the application is made.

A different approach is followed in the **region of Campania**, where LTC is financed by the National Fund (FNNA) to cover severe disability. A cash benefit is provided to a family member acting as *caregiver*, or to a private institution acting as a proxy, in order to preserve the health of the beneficiary and help the welfare condition of the entire household.[61] The target group includes individuals who are affected by severe disability and in need-of-care for 24 hours a day. The assessment process is carried out on the basis of a multidimensional scale known as "SVaMA-form". This is based on a comprehensive set of measures which evaluates the limitations of the applicant ranging from mobility impairments and limitations in functional abilities to mental disorders ("Barthel Index"). The Barthel scale used in Campania generates ten outcomes, each of them is assigned a score which is increasing in the loss of autonomy. In particular, for each outcome five scores are available, as summarised in Table 3.25. It is worth noting that the Barthel scale does not comprise iADL tasks. However, it also includes the economic conditions and the housing arrangements of the household (Pilotto et al., 2013).[62]

Table 3.25 Campania's Barthel assessment of need (vulnerability scores in brackets)

Outcome	*Level 1*	*Level 2*	*Level 3*	*Level 4*	*Level 5*
Bathing self	(0) Able to wash him/herself without help	(1) Needs supervision (transferring, water temperature)	(2) Needs assistance for transferring or washing or to dry off	(3) Needs assistance in washing above and below waist	(4) Must be fully supported in washing
Personal toilet	(0) Performs face-care, tooth brushing, combing, shaving	(1) Needs minimal help before and/or after the tasks	(2) Needs help for one or more tasks	(4) Needs help for all tasks	(5) Unable to perform personal toilet
Dressing	(0) Able to dress and undress without help	(2) Needs minimal assistance	(5) Needs some assistance to dress/undress	(8) Needs full assistance to dress above and below the waist	(8) Must be fully supported in dressing, non cohoperative
Walking on level surface	(0) Autonomous in moving, with or without appliances	(3) Needs supervision to boost confidence	(7) Need help to reach and/or appliances	(12) Needs help for all movements or transfers	(15) Not able to move autonomously
Ascend and descend stairs	(0) Able to ascend and descend one flight of stairs	(2) Needs supervision to boost confidence	(5) Needs supervision and is unable to use appliances	(8) Needs help for ascend and descend	(8) Unable to ascend and descend
Transferring from chair to bed and return	(0) Autonomous in transferring without help or appliances	(3) Needs supervision to boost confidence	(7) Need help for at least one move or transfer	(12) Needs help for all movements or transfers	(15) Must be moved, non-cooperative
Using the toilet	(0) Able to use the toilet, including (un) dressing and cleaning, without help	(2) Needs supervision	(5) Needs help for two among: Going to the toilet, dressing, cleaning	(8) Needs help in going to the toilet, dressing and cleaning	(8) Fully dependent

(continued)

Table 3.25 (continued)

Outcome	*Level 1*	*Level 2*	*Level 3*	*Level 4*	*Level 5*
Controlling bowel	(0) Able to retain stool	(2) Accidentally incontinent for stool	(5) Incontinent for stool during the night	(8) Incontinent for stool	(8) Incontinent, needs help for dealing with catheter
Controlling bladder	(0) Able to retain urine	(2) Accidentally incontinent for urine	(5) Incontinent for urine during the night	(8) Incontinent for urine	(8) Incontinent, needs help for dealing with catheter
Eating	(0) Able to eat and drink independently	(2) Needs help before eating or drinking	(5) Able to eat but needs supervision in side activities	(8) Needs assistance while eating or drinking	(8) Totally dependent for eating or drinking

Source: Regional resolution DGR 323/2012

Table 3.26 The Barthel scale in the SVaMA assessment procedure of the Campania Region

Limitation in	*Assessment values*	*Assigned value*	*SHARE tasks*
Feeding	0/2/5/8/10	8	Eating (+cutting up your food)
Bathing self	0/1/2/4/5	4	Bathing or showering
Personal toilet	0/1/2/4/5	2	Bathing or showering
Dressing	0/2/5/8/10	8	Dressing (+putting on shoes and socks)
Controlling bowels	0/2/5/8/10	–	–
Controlling bladder	0/2/5/8/10	8	Incontinence or involuntary loss of urine
Getting on and off toilet	0/2/5/8/10	8	Using the toilet (+getting up or down)
Moving from chair to bed and return	0/3/7/12/15	12	Getting in or out of bed
Walking on level surface	0/3/7/12/15	12	Walking across a room
Ascend and descend stairs	0/2/5/8/10	8	Climbing one flight of stairs

In order to build the Barthel score in the SHARE sample, we assumed that a limitation recorded in SHARE corresponds to the fourth-highest score in the Barthel scale, consistent with the approach followed throughout this chapter for categorical measures of vulnerability (Table 3.26).[63]

Eligibility requires a minimum Barthel score of 55 ("Disabilità grave"), which corresponds to the "severe dependency" level entitling the recipient to a monthly cash benefit of €600 (for a period of 12 months). A Barthel score higher than 70 corresponds to "extremely high dependency" ("disabilità gravissima") and entitles to a monthly benefit of either €900 (for scores between 71 and 85, labelled as "intermediate need-of-care") or €1500 (scores higher than 85, labelled as "high need-of-care"). There is no means-testing and eligibility does not depend upon age (Table 3.27).

In the **Toscana region**, the main regional long-term care programme is the PAC (*Progetto per l'assistenza continua alla persona non autosufficiente*) introduced in 2010, which is yet of a different variety from the ones operating in the Bolzano Province and in Campania.[64] The PAC is financed by the *Fondo per la non autosufficienza* and encompasses both in-cash and in-kind benefits for adults older than 64, with the aim of favouring care within the home environment. The programme is means-

Table 3.27 Eligibility rules for Regione Campania's Assegno di Cura

Vulnerability category	*Overall Barthel score*	*Monthly cash benefit in Euro (2017)*
0	0–54	– (not eligible)
1—Severe dependency	55–70	€ 600
2—Extremely high dependency, intermediate need-of-care	71–85	€ 900
3—Extremely high dependency, high need-of-care	86–100	€ 1500

Source: Regional resolution DGR 261/2016

tested on the basis of household income.[65] Several home-care services are included in the PAC, ranging from nursing care by public medical professionals, to cash benefits in the form of vouchers, aimed at helping with the costs of hiring a private professional caregiver, to cash benefits or respite-care services for informal caregivers. The PAC is managed by the health authority at the district level: each district sets up a Multidisciplinary Evaluation Unit (UVM), including a doctor, a nurse and a welfare worker, who are responsible for the assessment of need of the older applicants and for the definition of a Personalised Plan of Assistance. Vulnerability is assessed by the UVM through a multidimensional approach that gathers individuals into five groups, representing five homogeneous levels of need-of-care. This is, to some extent, similar to the rationale of the French AGGIR scale (Sect. 3.4), allocating individuals with similar loss of autonomy and equivalent need-of-care. The Toscana's PAC assesses individuals' limitations in three main dimensions: Basic Activities of Daily Living (BADL); Cognitive Impairment; Mood and Behaviour. The BADL is a Katz-adapted list of activities-of-daily living included in the Minimum Data Set for Home Care (MDS-HC) assessment method.[66] It has seven items, compared with Katz's six, since the "mobility" task is split into a "transferring" activity (as in the Katz ADL scale), a "moving when in bed" and a "moving around house" activity. Each activity is evaluated on a five-step scale, from 0 (independence) to 4 (full assistance required) according to the need-of-care required by the applicant in the last seven days, as illustrated in Table 3.28. When matching the BADL assessment to the SHARE respondents, we assign a score of 3 (over 4) for each reported limitation.

Table 3.28 Assessment of need for BADL, Toscana's PAC

Limitations	*Description*	*Original evaluation*	*SHARE tasks (yes/no)*	*Assigned value*
Bathing	Needs help with bathing more than one part of the body, getting in or out of the tub or shower	From 0 to 4	Bathing or showering	3 out of 4
Dressing	Needs help with dressing self or needs to be completely dressed	From 0 to 4	Dressing	3 out of 4
Use of WC	Needs help transferring to the toilet, cleaning self or uses bedpan or commode	From 0 to 4	Using the toilet	3 out of 4
Moving	Needs help in moving around the house, even when using mobility aids	From 0 to 4	Walking across a room	3 out of 4
Transferring	Needs help in moving from bed to chair or requires a complete transfer	From 0 to 4	Transferring: Getting in or out of bed	3 out of 4
Moving in bed	Needs help in changing position when in bed	From 0 to 4	Transferring: Getting in or out of bed	3 out of 4
Nutrition	Needs partial or total help with feeding or requires parenteral feeding	From 0 to 4	Eating	3 out of 4

Notes: Adapted from Profili, Razzanelli, Soli, and Marini (2009). Supervision refers to a need of supervision for three or more times a week; light dependency refers to a need of light physical-help for three or more times; heavy dependency refers to a need of heavy physical-help for three or more times; full dependency refers to constant need for help. Evaluation codes: 0—independence; 1—supervision only: 2—light dependency; 3—heavy dependency; 4—full dependency

Three degrees of dependency in BADL are then identified, according to the number and the intensity of the BADL limitations experienced by the individual (Table 3.29).

Cognitive impairment is measured through the application of Eric Pfeiffer's Short Portable Mental Status Questionnaire and classifies patients as "non impaired or lightly impaired", "moderately impaired" or "severely impaired".[67] The questionnaire includes questions on time orientation (current day of the week, current date in full), space orientation (name of the current location, phone number), age and birthdate, knowledge of the current prominent people, own mother's maiden name, and a math question. The answers are then transformed into an overall score

Table 3.29 Definition of dependency in BADL, Toscana's PAC

Dependency in BADL	*Description*	*BADL scale*
Light	Full dependency in 2 BADL *or* light/heavy dependency in 3 BADL	At least 8
Moderate	Full dependency in 3 BADL *or* light/heavy dependency in 4+ BADL	At least 15
Severe	Heavy dependency in roughly all BADL	At least 21

Notes: Adapted from Profili et al. (2009).

Table 3.30 Toscana's cognitive evaluation and SHARE

Assigned value	*SHARE tasks*
Light	Disoriented in time (day, week, month, year): Cannot answer one or two
Moderate	Disoriented in time (day, week, month, year): Cannot answer three
Severe	Disoriented in time (day, week, month, year): Cannot answer four

from 0 points to 2 points. In SHARE, we use the "orientation" question as summarised in Table 3.30.

Mood- and Behaviour-assessment follow the guidelines from MDS-HC. For example, mood assessment consists in a list of questions about whether the patient exhibits: (i) a feeling of sadness, depression or death wishes; (ii) persistent anger with self or others; (iii) expressions of what appears to be unrealistic fears; (iv) repetitive health complaints (obsessive concerns); (v) repetitive anxious complaints; (vi) sad, pained, worried facial expressions; (vii) recurrent crying, tearfulness; (viii) withdrawal from activities of interest; (ix) reduced social interaction; instances when client exhibited behavioural symptoms. Depending on the number of mood and behavioural disturbances, an individual is categorised as "lightly disturbed", "moderately disturbed" or "severely disturbed". As for the matching with SHARE, we consider individuals affected by behavioural problems respondents who score a value of 4 or more in the EURO-D, which corresponds to a clinically significant level of depression.[68]

Five groups of vulnerability are built by combining the BADL status, the cognitive status and the mood/behavioural status. Group 5 corresponds to the worse BADL status together with severe cognitive impairment and severe behavioural disorders, while group 1 amounts to a light

Table 3.31 ISO-vulnerability groups, Toscana's PAC

	BADL limitations								
ISO-group	*Light*			*Moderate*			*Severe*		
	Mood/behav. impairment			*Mood/behav. impairment*			*Mood/behav. impairment*		
Cognitive impairment	L	M	S	L	M	S	L	M	S
L	1	2	3	2	3	4	4	4	5
M	2	2	3	3	3	4	4	4	5
S	3	3	4	3	4	5	4	5	5

Notes: Adapted from Profili et al. (2009) and Visca et al. (2012). *L* light, *M* moderate, *S* severe

deficit in one of the three dimensions. It is worth noting that the region of Sardegna has recently legislated in favour of the adoption of the same vulnerability matrix (with functionality being measured through the Modified Barthel Index, see Appendix A.2).[69] Table 3.31 explains in detail how the iso-groups are defined.[70]

The final eligibility for PAC depends on age, income and on the ISO-vulnerability group assessed by the UVM, as shown in Table 3.32.

The minimum age is 65 years old. The minimum ISO category is 3, even though the UVM can, in principle, decide to allow some benefit for individuals in groups 1 and 2.[71] The amount of the in-kind or the in-cash allowance is means-tested: individuals with yearly household income above €25000 will not receive any benefit.[72] Moreover, they depend on the ISO-vulnerability categorisation, as shown in Table 3.33.

In our matching with SHARE, a respondent is classified as being in ISO category 3 when she has at least: (i) light BADL dependency and both behavioural and cognitive limitations; (ii) moderate BADL dependency and *either* behavioural or cognitive limitations; and (iii) moderate BADL dependency.

Finally, in the **Veneto region** we also find LTC provisions aimed at favouring home care.[73] The funds are allocated to the local health authorities and are earmarked for individuals who are not autonomous and are in need of constant care. Provisions are cash benefits or welfare-care provisions, but support for caregivers is also given. As from 2013, the actual health-related home provisions are part of the ICD (*Impegnativa di Cura Domiciliare*) which can be in cash or in kind for activities of daily living

Table 3.32 Toscana's PAC eligibility rules

Individual characteristics	*Eligibility requirements*
Age	At least 65 years old
Economic resources	Yearly household income lower than € 25,000
Health	ISO-GROUP 3 or higher

Table 3.33 Monetary allowances, Toscana's PAC

ISO-group	*Minimum–Maximum allowance*
3	[€ 80–€ 120]
4	[€ 170–€ 310]
5	[€ 260–€ 450]

given directly to the beneficiary or to a relative.[74] These provisions are also classified into ICDb (low impairment), ICDm (medium impairment) and ICDa (high impairment), the average benefit is €120, €400 per month for either a low or a medium limitation, while it can also vary for a severe case of limitation.

There exists a multidimensional assessment unit (*Unità di Valutazione Multidimensionale Distrettuale*, UVMD) which has to establish the health and welfare conditions through a SVAMA form, similarly to the Campania region. However, the Veneto region sets an explicit eligibility threshold for eligibility, which involves all the dimensions included in the SVaMA, including: adequate support and care from the family (*carer sighted*); a low-income condition according to the ISEE level of income of €23,900 (if a home-owner) or €16,700 (for non-home-owners).[75]

As per the health assessment procedure, the SVaMA scale comprises several dimensions, which are summarised in Table 3.34. We will now briefly describe what outcomes are included in each dimension, and how we establish a proper correspondence with the SHARE data.

The cognitive evaluation relevant for eligibility is assessed through the Short Portable Mental Status Questionnaire (Pfeiffer, 1975), as applied in Toscana, and it is summarised in Table 3.35.[76]

The evaluation of behavioural disorders is performed by the UVMD without a predefined assessment scale, and leads to the assignment of a score between 1 and 3. The first level corresponds to either the absence (or only a mild level) of disorders, the intermediate score of 2 corresponds

Table 3.34 The "simplified" SVaMA assessment scale for Veneto's ICDb programme

Dimensions	*Evaluation*		
Cognition	Lucid	Confused	Highly confused/ stuporous
Score for SVaMA	1	2	3
Behavioural disorders	None	Moderate	Severe
Score for SVaMA	1	2	3
Barthel functional scale	Autonomous	Dependent	Fully dependent
Score for SVaMA	1	2	3
Barthel mobility scale	Autonomous	Needs assistance	Unable to move
Score for SVaMA	1	2	3
Social network support	Inadequate	Partially assisted	Well-assisted
Score for SVaMA	1	2	3
Need for medical assistance	Low	Intermediate	High
Score for SVaMA	1	2	3

Source: Regional resolution DGR 1338/2013

Table 3.35 Veneto's cognitive evaluation and SHARE

Assigned value	*SHARE tasks*
1 (Light)	Disoriented in time (day, week, month, year): Cannot answer one or two
2 (Moderate)	Disoriented in time (day, week, month, year): Cannot answer three
3 (Severe)	Disoriented in time (day, week, month, year): Cannot answer four

to a condition where supervision and support is needed, but not on a continuous basis; finally, a score of 3 indicates that the subject can cause harm to herself or to others and physical and pharmacological interventions are needed. In matching this dimension with SHARE (Table 3.36), we follow the same strategy implemented throughout this chapter, and label as having (at least) "moderate" limitation those respondents with an EURO-D score of 4 (or higher).

The components of the Barthel Functional and Mobility scale are the same as those adopted by the legislations in the Campania region, as per Table 3.25. The correspondence with SHARE is illustrated in Table 3.37.

The SVaMA includes a dimension labelled as "Social network support" (*Supporto della rete sociale*), where the UVMD unit evaluates whether (and the extent to which) the older person's social network is able to meet

Table 3.36 Behavioural evaluation Veneto's ICD programme and SHARE

Assigned value	*SHARE tasks*
1 (No/mild issues)	EURO-D score lower than 4
2 (Moderate)	EURO-D score equal of higher than 4
3 (Severe)	–

Table 3.37 The Veneto's Barthel scale (Functional and Mobility) and SHARE

Limitation in	*Assessment values*	*Assigned value*	*SHARE tasks*
Functional			
Feeding	0/2/5/8/10	8	Eating (+cutting up your food)
Bathing self	0/1/2/4/5	4	Bathing or showering
Personal toilet	0/1/2/4/5	2	Bathing or showering
Dressing	0/2/5/8/10	8	Dressing (+ putting on shoes and socks)
Controlling bowels	0/2/5/8/10	–	–
Controlling bladder	0/2/5/8/10	8	Incontinence or involuntary loss of urine
Using the toilet	0/2/5/8/10	8	Using the toilet (+ getting up or down)
Mobility			
Moving from chair to bed and return	0/3/8/12/15	12	Getting in or out of bed
Walking on level surface	0/3/8/12/15	12	Walking across a room
Ascend and descend stairs	0/2/5/8/10	8	Climbing one flight of stairs

Source: Regional resolution DGR 2961/2012

her demands for care. The assessment includes a list of ADL and iADL, as well as the need for psychological support, and day and night supervision. For each outcome four levels of evaluation are possible: "autonomous" (the subject does not need support), or—if the subject is not autonomous in the specific task—"adequate", "partially adequate" and "inadequate". Each evaluation carries a specific score, and the overall sum of scores allows a person to be categorised as "well-assisted", "partially assisted" or "not adequately assisted". It is interesting to notice how, in the original SVaMA scale, the "not adequately assisted" category is assigned the highest scores, while the opposite it true in the "modified SVaMA" which is adopted for determining the eligibility to the entry-level programme

ICDb. Indeed, Table 3.34 illustrates how the "well-assisted" individual gets 3 points for the overall evaluation, while the "inadequately" assisted gets only 1 point. This modification has been added to incentivise good practices and higher intensity by the informal caregivers, given that an adequate social networking has been introduced as a requisite for ICDb eligibility. In order to match this dimension with SHARE data, we exploit the information on both functional abilities and the assistance received by the informal network (e.g., spouse, offspring, friends, neighbours) for the same set of ADL or iADL, as summarised in Table 3.38. Since SHARE does not allow for a quantification of the amount of informal care received (no information is available for the care coming from household members, while an ordinal qualitative response is available for external help) nor for a specific link between the assistance right received and a specific limitation, we follow a prudent approach: we label as well-assisted those who suffer from at least one ADL or iADL limitation and claim to receive some support from either a household member or an external caregiver, while those who receive help only from one of the two sources are labelled as "partially assisted". Respondents not receiving any care are labelled as "not adequately assisted". Informal assistance from outside the household occurring with a frequency lower than monthly ("less often") is not considered.

The last dimension of the "simplified" SVaMA assessment involves an overall evaluation of an individual's "need for medical care". Outcomes

Table 3.38 Evaluation of social network support within Veneto's ICD eligibility rules

Level	*Score*	*Criteria*	*Eligibility requirements*
Well-assisted	3	Functional limitations	Having either ADL or iADL limitations
		Support	Receiving support from both inside and outside the household
Partially assisted	2	Functional limitations	Having either ADL or iADL limitations
		Support	Receiving support only from either outside or inside the household
Not adequately assisted	1	Functional limitations	–
		Support	Receiving no support from any informal caregiver

Table 3.39 Evaluation of social network support within Veneto's ICD eligibility rules

Need for medical care	*Score*	*Criteria*
Low	1	A score of 2 in less than two dimensions among Cognition, Behaviour, Functioning, Mobility
Intermediate	2	A score of 2 in at least two dimensions among Cognition, Behaviour, Functioning, Mobility
High	3	–

involved the likelihood of rehabilitation from current functional limitations, nursing-care needs (e.g., for diabetes drugs, tracheostomy, oxygen therapy, catheters, monitoring of fluid balance, food, and vital signs), risk of pressure sores (through the Exton Smith Index involving physical and mental conditions, activity and mobility, incontinence). Depending on the score assigned in each outcome, individuals are labelled as having a "low", "intermediate" or "high" need for medical care. When not directly available in SHARE, we define as having "intermediate" need for medical care those obtaining a score of 2 (out of 3) in at least two of the first four dimensions in the SVaMA assessment (Cognition, Behaviour, Functioning, Mobility) (Table 3.39).

Table 3.40 summarises the eligibility conditions for the Veneto programmes. As we are interested in the minimum level of objective vulnerability that gives access to LTC benefits, in the following empirical chapters we will operationalise the rules for the ICDb entry-level programme, which is based on the "simplified SVaMA" summarised in Table 3.34.

3.7 The Spanish SAAD

In order to analyse the Spanish LTC system one needs to separate the two regimes emerging from the introduction of the *Ley de Dependencia* in 2006, which regulates formal long-term care programmes both in the form of in-kind services and in cash benefits.[77]

The former Spanish system was highly decentralised and characterised by "regional LTC services", where the access to publicly funded long-term assistance was based on region-specific assessments of need and relied on local resources. The social security system provided assistance in the form of benefits for those with a high degree of dependency, cash allowances within the non-contributory disability pension and family benefits

Table 3.40 Eligibility rules for Veneto's ICD programmes

Programme	*Monetary amount*	*Criteria*	*Eligibility requirements*
ICDb	€ 120	Economic resources	ISEE "sociosanitario" lower than € 16,700 net of real wealth, or lower than € 23,000 including real wealth
		Health	SVaMA ("simplified version") score 5+
ICDm	€ 400	Economic resources	ISEE "sociosanitario" lower than € 16,700 net of real wealth, or lower than € 23,000 including real wealth
		Health	SVaMA score 54+
ICDa	€ 800[a]	Economic resources	ISEE "sociosanitario" lower than € 60,000 net of real wealth
		Health	SVaMA score 54+

Sources: DGR 1047/2015 and DGR 1338/2013

[a]The amount is modifiable according to the individuals' needs and the agreed care plan

for those with disabled children. The supply of social services has been inadequate to meet the needs of dependent population, and characterised by a high level of heterogeneity among regions which led to a large expansion of privately provided programmes (OECD, 2011).

To harmonise this complex legislative setting, the Spanish government enacted a new Law aimed at "*configuring a network for public use that integrated on a coordinated basis, both public and private centres and services*" (Jiménez-Martín & Prieto, 2010). The new programme was called "*Promoción de la Autonomía Personal y Atención a las personas en situación de dependencia*" (System for Promotion of Personal Autonomy and Assistance for Persons in a Situation of Dependency, SAAD). The law defined "dependency" as *the permanent state in which persons require the care of others to perform basic activities of daily living, for reasons derived from age, illness or disability and related to the lack or loss of physical, mental, intellectual or sensorial autonomy* and introduced a standardised procedure of assessment at the national level. The current evaluation process is carried out by an autonomous administration operating in the applicant's residence and it is the same throughout the country. The degrees and levels of dependency are established by using an assessment scale (Table 3.41) approved by the Territorial Council of the System for Autonomy and Care for Dependency.

Table 3.41 Assessment of need in the Spanish SAAD

Activities—Tasks	*Weight*	*SHARE tasks*
Eating and drinking	**16.8 (10)**	Eating (+ cutting up your food)
Recognise e/o reach the food served	0.25	|
Cutting up food	0.2	|
Using cutlery	0.3	|
Putting a glass to mouth	0.25	|
Control of physical needs	**14.8 (7)**	Using the toilet (+ getting up or down)
Go to the appropriate place	0.2	|
Dressing and undressing	0.15	|
Adopting the right posture	0.3	|
Cleaning oneself	0.35	|
Bathing	**8.8 (8)**	Bathing or showering
Turning on and turning off taps	0.15	|
Washing hands	0.2	|
Using shower or bath tub	0.15	|
Washing lower part of the body	0.25	|
Washing upper part of the body	0.25	|
Other personal tasks	**2.9 (2)**	Bathing or showering
Combing hair	0.3	|
Cutting nails	0.15	|
Washing hair	0.25	|
Brushing teeth	0.3	|
Dressing	**11.9 (11.6)**	Dressing (+ putting on shoes and socks)
Recognise e/o reach clothes and shoes	0.15	|
Putting on shoes	0.1	|
Doing up buttons	0.15	|
Dressing upper part of the body	0.3	|
Dressing lower part of the body	0.3	|
Maintaining health	**2.9 (11)**	
Request therapeutic assistance	0.15	Taking medications
Applying therapeutic measures	0.1	Taking medications
Avoiding indoor risks	0.25	Walking across a room
Avoiding outdoor risks	0.25	Walking across a room
Distress call	0.25	Making telephone calls
Maintaining health 2	**9.4 (2)**	–
Changing position from lying to sitting on the bed	0.1	Getting in or out of bed
Sitting	0.15	Sitting for about 2 h
Getting up from a chair	0.1	Getting up from a chair after sitting for long periods
Standing up	0.15	Getting in or out of bed

(*continued*)

Table 3.41 (continued)

Activities—Tasks	*Weight*	*SHARE tasks*
Sitting down on a chair	0.1	Getting in or out of bed
Changing posture from a sitting position	0.1	Getting in or out of bed
Changing posture from bed	0.1	Getting in or out of bed
Changing centre of gravity of body in the bed	0.2	Getting in or out of bed
Moving inside home	**12.3 (12.1)**	–
Movements related dressing	0.25	Dressing (+ putting on shoes and socks)
Movements related eating	0.15	Eating (+ cutting up your food)
Movements related washing	0.1	Bathing or showering
Movements not related to self-care	0.25	Walking across a room
Access to all settings of the rooms	0.1	Walking across a room
Access to all rooms	0.15	Walking across a room
Moving outside home	**12.2 (12.9)**	–
Going out	0.25	Walking across a room
Walking around the house/building	0.25	Walking across a room
Walking short distances in known places	0.2	Walking across a room
Walking short distances in unknown places	0.15	Walking across a room *or* Using a map to figure out how to get around in a strange place
Walking long distances in known places	0.1	Walking across a room
Walking long distances in unknown places	0.05	Walking across a room *or* Using a map to figure out how to get around in a strange place
Housekeeping	**8 (8)**	
Cooking	0.45	Preparing a hot meal
Shopping (for food)	0.25	Shopping for groceries
Cleaning the house	0.2	Doing work around the house or garden
Washing clothes	0.1	Doing work around the house or garden
Only for patients with a mental illness or cognitive impairment:		
Making decisions	**(15.4)**	Disoriented in time (day, week, month, year): Cannot answer three or more

Source: Real Decreto 174/2011, Ministerio de Sanidad, Politica Social e Igualdad "BOE", No. 42, 18/02/2011

Similarly to the Czech Republic, the Spanish ranking scale consists of ten distinct limitations to activities and, in turn, each activity includes a set of specific tasks. An additional activity (making decisions) is included only for individuals who suffer from mental disorders or cognitive impairment. Moreover, for this specific group of vulnerable persons the ranking scale assigns different weights to each activity (they are reported in parenthesis). The Spanish legislation allows for different degrees of *loss of autonomy* for each of the aforementioned tasks. The need of support can be *special*, *full* or *partial*, to which is assigned a coefficient of 1, 0.95 or 0.9 respectively. These support coefficients must be multiplied to the coefficient of the task in which the limitations is experienced. E.g., if an individual has *full* limitations in cooking, she will be assigned a score of 0.45×0.95 within the dimension *Housekeeping* (Table 3.42).

The final score is the sum of the weights of the tasks for which the individual has difficulty, multiplied by the degree of supervision required and the weight assigned to that activity:

Score = $\sum$(Weight of the task performed with difficulty × Degree of supervision required in the specific task × Weight of the corresponding activity)

To summarise, the Spanish assessment scale involves ten *Activities* (plus one for mentally impaired individuals). Each activity comprises several *tasks*. Each Activity carries a weight (bold in Table 3.41, e.g., 16.8 for Eating and drinking). Each task has a coefficient (bounded between 0 and 1), representing the share of the Activity's weight carried by that task (e.g., Cutting up food has the 20 per cent of the Eating and drinking

Table 3.42 Definitions for the need-of-support levels

Support coefficient			
0.9	*0.9*	*0.95*	*1*
Supervision	*Partial physical assistance*	*Maximum physical assistance*	*Special assistance*
If the dependent only needs a third person to prepare the necessary elements to perform the activity	When a third person has to participate actively	If the third person has to substitute the dependent individual in the execution of the activity	The dependent individual suffers behavioural disorders that hinder the provision of the task by the third person

weight). When an individual is mentally impaired, a further activity is considered, while the remaining ten are assigned a new weight (in parenthesis): e.g., for a mentally impaired individual the weight of the activity Eating and drinking is 10.

Since some of the tasks included in the SAAD assessment do not correlate directly with the SHARE dataset, we opted to adopt a prudential approach. For example, if we consider the task "moving *outdoor*" (which is an iADL) we use from SHARE the respondents' ability to "move *indoor*". Since we want to avoid overestimates of the dependency status, "moving *indoor*" is a more stringent requirement than walking *outdoor* and will provide a conservative estimate of this limitation. As usual when it comes to the intensity of the limitation we impute a need-of-support equal to 0.9 as a prudential estimate. To sum up, in our matching with SHARE, the SAAD vulnerability score is constituted by the sum of the coefficient assigned to each task (in which the respondents reports a loss of autonomy), each being multiplied by the support-coefficient 0.9 and furthermore by the weight assigned to the corresponding activity. E.g., an individual who reports only a limitation in cooking will have a total score of $0.45 \times 0.9 \times 8$.

The ranking scale identifies three degrees of dependency: (i) *moderate dependency*, when the person needs help to perform various basic daily living activities at least once a day; (ii) *severe dependency*, when the person needs help in order to perform various basic daily living activities two or three times a day; and (iii) *high dependency*, when the person needs help to perform various basic daily living activities several times a day and due to the total loss of physical, mental, intellectual or sensorial autonomy, she needs permanent support of another person.

Within each of the three degrees, the ranking scale distinguishes two levels of dependency on the basis of the person's autonomy and on the intensity of care required. The first level corresponds to those individuals who can perform the activity without the direct help of a third person, whereas the second level refers to those situations in which the dependent individual needs some type of specific help. Table 3.43 shows the ranking scale used for the determination of the degree of dependency (Fernanda Gutierrez, Jimenez-Martin, Vegas Sanchez, & Vilaplana, 2010; Jiménez-Martín & Prieto, 2010).

Once the assessment-of-need procedure is complete, the dependent person is entitled to receive formal care by means of services and benefits that are matched to the degree and level of their dependency (Individual

Table 3.43 Degrees and levels of dependency (score) in the Spanish SAAD

Degree	*Score*	*Level*
High dependence	90–100	Level 2
High dependence	75–89	Level 1
Severe dependence	65–74	Level 2
Severe dependence	50–64	Level 1
Moderate dependence	40–49	Level 2
Moderate dependence	25–39	Level 1
Not dependent	0–24	

Source: Fernanda Gutierrez et al. (2010)

Care Programme) (Fernanda Gutierrez et al., 2010). The assessment of needs, the prescription of assistance and the management of the care allowances are carried out directly by the public administrations.

Different types of in-kind services are offered: the "Home help service", which includes housework and other services related to home needs (cleaning, bathing, cooking, etc.), the personal care and related services in performing daily activities. The 2006 law has introduced a specific regulation in terms of home-care hours received by month, according to the level and the grade of dependency of vulnerable individuals (see Table 3.44).

Concerning the cash benefits, three types of allowances are available: (i) allowance for the care recipient to hire services. This benefit is meant for the care recipient to hire services through private centres (with accreditation), when public services are not available; (ii) allowance for the care recipient also receiving informal care. In order to collect the benefit, the informal carer has to be a relative of the dependent person, except in the case that services are unavailable in the area (in this situation, the informal carer must be a neighbour residing in the same municipalities, or nearby); (iii) allowance for personal assistance. This benefit is meant for individuals having a high degree of disability (Degree III) to hire personal help in order to provide them with access to work and education and help in daily activities.

All cash allowances are means-tested and depend on cost, or on hours of care for the allowance towards informal carers (OECD 2011; Fernanda Gutierrez et al. 2010) (Table 3.45).

It is useful to point out two relevant aspects of the SAAD assessment process. The Spanish system places the emphasis on the intensity of support needed and the tasks for which care is required. The vulnerability

Table 3.44 Home-care hours, Spanish SAAD

Intensive home care	
Level of dependency	*Home care (h/month)*
High dependence. Level 2	70–90
High dependence. Level 1	55–70
Severe dependence. Level 2	40–55
Severe dependence. Level 1	30–40
Moderate dependence. Level 2	21–30
Moderate dependence. Level 1	12–20

Non-intensive home care	
Level of dependency	*Home care (h/month)*
High dependence. Level 2	Up to 45
High dependence. Level 1	Up to 35
Severe dependence. Level 2	Up to 28
Severe dependence. Level 1	Up to 20

Source: Fernanda Gutierrez et al. (2010)

Table 3.45 Monetary allowances and levels of dependence

Levels of dependence	*Allowance for the care recipient to hire services*	*Allowance for the care recipient receiving informal care*	*Allowance for personal assistance*
High—level 2	833.96	520.69	833.96
High—level 1	625.47	416.08	625.47
Severe—level 2	426.18	337.25	Not available
Severe—level 1	401.20	300.90	Not available
Moderate—level 2	300	180	Not available
Moderate—level 1	Not implemented yet	Not implemented yet	Not implemented yet

Source: Fernanda Gutierrez et al. (2010)

assessment is highly detailed with respect to all activities included in the scale, and special attention is paid to those individuals who have limitations in eating/drinking tasks or in performing daily living tasks such as dressing and undressing and cleaning oneself. The dependency status is evaluated, for each limitation, by using a weighted scale, in which different weights have been assigned to each specific task. Interestingly, the Spanish ranking scale assigns different activity coefficients (and an additional activity: *making decisions*) to those individuals who have a difficulty in performing tasks due to some cognitive or intellectual challenges. Its focus on mental aspects of frailty is in line with the WHO bio-psychological perspective (WHO, 2002).

From an empirical point of view, it is useful to point out that the reform was implemented in steps, with the individuals in the highest levels of vulnerability being given priority. Although the new system was supposed to be fully operational by 2015, delays were imposed by the austerity policies which generated a "dependency limbo" category of applicants, i.e., individuals who were assessed as eligible and yet not receiving any benefit (Peña-Longobardo, Oliva-Moreno, García-Armesto, & Hernández-Quevedo, 2016).

3.8 Adults' Social Care in England and Wales

The LTC system for older adults in England and Wales encompasses several different services, ranging from in-kind or in-cash home-care (both in the form of social or health care) administered by local authorities and the Department of Health, to monetary benefits (Attendance Allowance) issued by the Department of Work and Pensions, and housing services (run by local authorities and the Department of Communities and Local Government). The former also implement different levels of means-testing and needs-testing. Providers may be local authority social services, community-level health services, as well as profit and non-profit sector home-care/day-care centres, residential-care and nursing homes (Comas-Herrera, Pickard, Wittenberg, Malley, & King, 2010). The recently implemented Care Act of 2014 incentivised a more comprehensive provision of information and advice by the local authorities about care and support services.[78]

If an older individual is deemed eligible to receive public support services, she will be given the choice whether to opt for an in-kind or an in-cash benefit. The latter, also called "direct payments", are meant to widen the choice and control over the care providers, and enhance the level of control of the beneficiary. The utilisation of benefits is restricted, e.g., to the hiring of personal assistants or compensation of informal caregivers, and in any case to the purchase of services or goods that meet the assessed needs of the person. To this end, social services perform a review of the care plans at least once a year. Since 2011, all eligible care beneficiaries are provided with a "personal budget" which enables them to choose a direct payment or to let the local authority manage the budget on behalf of the user. The latter is the most widely adopted solution in the recent years (Gori & Fernandez, 2015), yet mixed packages of care (i.e., some direct payment and some support arranged by the council) are possible.[79]

Access to public care support goes through a need-assessment process carried out by local authorities. Before the introduction of the Care Act 2014, the assessment process varied greatly at the local level, the introduction of the guidelines by the Department of Health aimed at "Prioritising need in the context of Putting People First: A whole system approach to eligibility for social care", also referred to as Fair Access to Care Services (SCIE, 2015). Although the Care Act 2014 emphasises that the assessment process should be person-centred and flexible, to reflect the wishes of the older person as well as their needs and circumstances, it clearly sets out the dimensions of loss of autonomy that should be evaluated. It also states that "the process should consider all of the adult's care and support needs, regardless of any support being provided by a carer", which must not influence the eligibility determination, therefore constituting a *carer's blind* approach.

The outcomes included in the assessment of needs are summarised in Table 3.46. The set of variables draws from both the ADL and the iADL taxonomy, even though the correspondence is somewhat complex at times because some aggregations are performed. In particular, the tasks which are included refer to: managing and maintaining nutrition (whether the adult has access to food and drink to maintain nutrition, and is able to prepare and consume the food and drink); maintaining personal hygiene (ability to wash oneself and launder clothes); managing toilet needs (ability to access and use a toilet); being appropriately clothed (ability to dress oneself and to be appropriately dressed); being able to make use of the home safely (ability to move around the home safely, and accessing the property); maintaining a habitable home environment (whether the condition of the adult's home is sufficiently clean and maintained to be safe); developing and maintaining family or other personal relationships (whether the adult is lonely or isolated, either because her needs prevent her from maintaining the personal relationships they have or because her needs prevent them from developing new relationships); accessing and engaging in work, training, education or volunteering (whether the adult has an opportunity to apply themselves and contribute to society through work,

Table 3.46 Assessment of need for adults with care and support needs, Care Act 2014

Limitation	*Evaluation (yes/no)*	*Assigned value*	*SHARE tasks (being unable to: yes/no)*
Managing and maintaining nutrition	1	1	Eating (+cutting up your food) *or* Preparing a hot meal
Maintaining personal hygiene	1	1	Bathing or showering
Managing toilet needs	1	1	Using the toilet (+ getting up or down)
Being appropriately clothed	1	1	Dressing (+ putting on shoes and socks)
Being able to make use of the adult's home safely	1	1	Walking across a room
Maintaining a habitable home environment	1	1	Doing work around the house *or* Managing money, such as paying bills and keeping track of expenses
Developing and maintaining family or other personal relationships	1	1	Making telephone calls while living alone *or* Disoriented in time (day, week, month, year): Cannot answer three or more, *or* EURO-D score equal to or higher than 4
Accessing and engaging in work, training, education or volunteering	1	–	–
Making use of necessary facilities or services in the local community, including public transport, and recreational facilities or services	1	1	Walking across a room *or* shopping for groceries
Carrying out any caring responsibilities the adult has for a child	1	–	–

Source: SCIE (2015)

training, education or volunteering, subject to their own wishes in this regard); making use of necessary facilities or services in the local community including public transport and recreational facilities or services (ability to use facilities as public transport, shops or recreational facilities); carrying out any caring responsibilities the adult has for a child (any parenting or other caring responsibilities of the person).

The assessment process evaluates whether or not an individual is "unable" to achieve the aforementioned outcomes. The Care Act statutory guidance highlights that such a condition includes multiple circumstances, like the inability to achieve the outcome without assistance (including inability to do so even when assistance is provided); ability to achieve the outcome without assistance but with significant pain, distress or anxiety; ability to achieve the outcome without assistance, but endangering one's own or other's health; ability to achieve the outcome without assistance but taking significantly longer than would normally be expected.

Most of the assessed outcomes have a close match both in the ELSA survey and the SHARE survey. We deal with outcomes which are obtained as a compound of multiple tasks, by replacing them with single tasks which are "substitutes". For example, the outcome "Developing and maintaining family or other personal relationships" refers to both the availability of partners with whom a relationship can be maintained, and the communication's ability of the older adult. Although our data lacks detailed information on loneliness, we are able to exploit both the respondents' answer to the "using the telephone ability" and the individual's cognitive abilities (expressed by the orientation variable).

The Care Act sets a minimum threshold for older adults' needs which all local authorities must comply with (although they can decide to meet needs that are not deemed to be eligible). Eligibility rules are stated in §6 of the Care and support statutory guidance.[80] Objectively vulnerable conditions "must relate to an impairment or illness, mean a person cannot achieve at least two outcomes in their day-to-day life, and that as a result there is a significant impact on their wellbeing. The eligibility determination must be made without regard to whether a carer might be meeting those needs at the given time" (SCIE, 2015). Three main features could be highlighted in the previous definition:

- The loss of autonomy is caused by a physical or mental impairment or illness and not by other circumstantial factors.
- As a result, the inability to achieve two or more of the aforementioned outcomes should emerge.
- Such a loss of autonomy leads (or is likely to lead) to a significant impact on the adult's well-being. Being 'wellbeing' a broad concept, the Care Act 2014 Statutory Guidance describes it as relating to concepts such as personal dignity; physical and mental health and emotional wellbeing; protection from abuse and neglect; control by

the individual over their day-to-day life; participation in work, education, training or recreation; social and economic wellbeing; domestic, family and personal domains; suitability of the individual's living accommodation; the individual's contribution to society. The Guidance specifies that all dimensions are equally important, and that no unique way of merging them into a single aggregate "concept" exists, thus emphasising the need for a holistic person-centred approach.

It is worth noticing that, in setting out a minimum threshold of two or more outcomes, the Care Act does not draw a precise distinction between ADL and iADL (AgeUK, 2017), and it specifies that no hierarchy exists among the eligibility outcomes, all being equally important (SCIE, 2015).

The care support for an eligible person receives is not entirely paid by the local authority: help is means-tested and the public covered amount depends on the degree of loss of autonomy, the individual's level of resources, and the type of care and support required. After performing an assessment of the claimant's finances, the local authority will determine how much to charge for its care services. The financial assessment focuses on a person's assets—both capital and income. The Care Act Statutory Guidance highlights that "a local authority has the discretion to choose whether or not to charge under section 14 of the Care Act following a person's needs assessment". For residential-care services ("care homes"), a financial limit, known as the 'upper capital limit', sets out the point at which a person is entitled to access local authority support to meet their eligible needs, and is set at £23,250 for the year 2017. A lower capital limit is set at £14,250, below which level the full cost is carried by the public authority.[81] For care settings which are not "residential", the aforementioned limits are simply minimums: local authorities have discretion to set their own higher capital limits if they wish, provided they are no lower than £23,250 for the upper limit and £14,250 for the lower limit.

A related, yet separate, form of monetary assistance is the Attendance Allowance, "a benefit for severely disabled people aged 65 or over who need help with personal care", which is tax-free and not means-tested. The benefit can come in two distinct amounts (for 2017/2018, £83.10 or £55.65 per week), depending on the extent of the loss of autonomy; there is no standardised assessment process, nor any clear-cut eligibility threshold. The Attendance Allowance can be spent with much lower constraints then the aforementioned Social Care direct payments, and is considered more as a compensation for disability rather than a payment to cover the costs of services (Comas-Herrera et al., 2010).

Finally, it is worth mentioning that in England and Wales the LTC system includes a substantial programme supporting informal caregivers, in the form of a cash benefit (Carer's Allowance) of £61.35 a week, with a one-off £10 Christmas bonus in December. Eligibility for such a benefit, issued by the Department for Work and Pensions, includes caring for at least 36 hours a week, being aged 16+, not earning over £116 a week, and caring for someone who gets a qualifying disability benefit (e.g., the Attendance Allowance). Furthermore, the Care Act 2014 has widened the opportunities for caregivers to receive support from local councils, which could include monetary or practical support, including respite care. Eligibility for support is regulated by the Care Act, and is based on an assessment which local authorities have a duty to perform, if any carer requests so.

Notes

1. The SHARE and ELSA surveys are described in detail in Chap. 4.
2. BGBl. (Bundesgesetzblatt) Nr. 110/1993, BGBl. II Nr. 37/1999.
3. BGBl. (Bundesgesetzblatt) II Nr. 37/1999.
4. BGBl. (Bundesgesetzblatt) Nr. 110/1993.
5. MISSOC (2014).
6. BMASK (2013a).
7. BMASK (2013a).
8. See also the Formular 703-25 "Determination of care requirement in addition to the medical opinion" in "Gutachterfibel-Bundespflegegeld (2009), Pensionsversicherungsanstalt (Pension Insurance Fund)", available on-line. See also the Formular 703-25 "Determination of care requirement in addition to the medical opinion" in the Pension Insurance Fund report Pensionsversicherungsanstalt (2009) available on-line (in German).
9. Compulsory Health Insurance Law, *Loi relative à l'assurance obligatoire soins de santé et indemnités*, 14 July 1994, M.B/B.S. 27/08/1994.
10. A comprehensive review on the Institutions that regulate LTC in Belgium is Willemé (2010).
11. This evaluation scale is labelled as BESADL (Belgian Evaluation scale for ADL) in Sermeus et al. (2010).
12. The *Allocation pour l'aide aux personnes âgées* (*Tegemoetkoming voor hulp aan bejaarden*) is regulated by the Royal Decree of 5 March 1990, M.B./B.S. 05/04/90.

13. See the webpage of the SPF Social Security (*Service public federal Sécurité sociale*), "L'allocation pour l'aide aux personnes âgées", available on-line at http://handicap.belgium.be/fr/mes-droits/allocation-aide-personnes-agees.htm
14. See the webpage of the FPS Social Security at http://handicap.belgium.be/fr/mes-droits/allocation-aide-personnes-agees.htm.
15. Further reference on the validity of APA scale can be found in Sermeus et al. (2010), p. 35.
16. The latter is only partially related to the iADL taxonomy by Lawton and Brody (1969), which included communication in the form of "being able to use the telephone" (see Appendix A.1).
17. Decree of 30 March 1999, B.S. (Belgisch Staatsblad) 28/05/1999.
18. SHARE respondents are asked not to report difficulties that are expected to last less than three months.
19. The SHARE questions ask: "In the last month, have you been sad or depressed", "Have you been irritable recently?"
20. The 12 disturbances are pessimism, depressed mood, suicidal thoughts, guilt, trouble sleeping, loss of interest, irritability, fatigue, inability to concentrate, lack of appetite, incapacity of enjoyment, tearfulness.
21. A review of the programmes regulated by MPSV can be found on-line at https://portal.mpsv.cz/soc as well as in MPSV (2009).
22. See the European Commission report (European Commission, 2013a) and Sowa (2010).
23. MPSV (2005).
24. Social Services Act No. 108/2006; Decree No. 505/2005, Implementing certain provisions of the Social Services Act.
25. Act No. 366/2011 (§9) amending the Social Services Act 108/2006. A brief review of the reform can be found online at a dedicated MPSV website http://socialnireforma.mpsv.cz/cs/23
26. For children below 18 years of age dependency is defined as follows: light dependency (limitations in three activities), medium dependency (limitations in five activities); heavy dependency (limitations in six to seven activities); very-heavy dependency (limitations in nine activities).
27. Source: https://www.finance.cz/479349-prumerny-duchod/
28. See Courbage and Roudaut (2010) and European Commission (2013b).
29. Decree n°97-427 du 28 avril 1997, Law n° 97-60 (24 January 1997), Décret no 2001-1084 du 20 novembre 2001, Décret no 2008-821 du 21 août 2008.
30. Further details can be found in the User Guide to the AGGIR scale 2008 by the CNAMTS (*Caisse nationale de l'assurance maladie des travailleurs salaries*—The French National Health Insurance Fund for Salaried Worker) at www.cnsa.fr/IMG/pdf/Guide_AGGIR_2008-2.pdf; in the documentation on the website of the Ministry of Health and Social Affairs (*Ministère*

des Affaires sociales et de la Santé) at http://www.social-sante.gouv.fr/IMG/pdf/fiche_1_grille_aggir_et_gir.pdf, as well as in https://www.service-public.fr/particuliers/vosdroits/F1229 and Dupourqué, Schoonveld, and Bushey (2012).

31. The AGGIR scale could, in principle, be included among the "analytic" assessment methods, since it comprises seventeen daily tasks above and beyond the ADL and the IADL taxonomies. As has just been highlighted, though, only eight of these tasks (the two items on mental deficits and the six ADL) actually contribute to determine an individual's vulnerability status.
32. (a) The individual performs the task spontaneously, habitually, completely and correctly alone. (b) The individual can perform the task alone, yet not spontaneously, and/or correctly and/or habitually and/or completely. (c) The individual cannot perform, requires assistance or must have someone else's help to do the activity.
33. Details are available in Dupourqué et al. (2012). A free AGGIR simulator is available at http://www.ibou.fr/aggir/
34. Syndicat National de Gérontologie Clinique (1994).
35. As mentioned before, only the first eight tasks determine an individual's eligibility status to LTC, while the remaining help to determine the amount and type of care that best suits each individual condition.
36. Articles L. 232-3/232-7, R. 232-7/232-14 of *Code de l'action sociale et des familles* (CFAS).
37. The *départment* is a level of government which lies between the region and the *arrondissement*.
38. Code de l'Action Sociale et des familles (CFAS), L 113-1/113-3, L. 231-1/231-6, R. 231/231-6, L. 313-1. CNAV Circular n° 2007-16 02/02/2007, CNAV Circular n° 2013-52 21/11/2013. Other references are available on-line at https://www.service-public.fr/particuliers/vosdroits/F245 and http://www.pour-les-personnes-agees.gouv.fr/beneficier-daides/laide-menagere-domicile
39. Except for GIR 6, which covers low dependency levels.
40. Monetary thresholds and contributions are valid throughout 2014. Further details on contributions and on the means-test are available on the French civil service website, at http://vosdroits.service-public.fr/particuliers/F245.xhtml
41. The Long-term Care Insurance is regulated in the 11th Book of the Social Code (*Buch des Sozialgesetzbuches*—SGB), available at http://www.gesetze-im-internet.de/sgb_11/index.html. Major recent modifications took place in 2008 (Long-term Care Further Development Act/Pflege-Weiterentwicklungsgesetz), 2012 (Law on Realignment of Care/Pflege-Neuausrichtungs-Gesetz), 2014 (Amendment to the 11th Book of Social

Code/*Änderung des Elften Buches Sozialgesetzbuch, 5. SGB XI-ÄndG, Änderungsgesetz*), and 2015 [see BMG (2015), Kalwitzki, Müller, Rothgang, Runte, and Unger (2015), and Bäcker (2016)].

42. Those German older adults under the Social Health Insurance (*Gesetzliche Krankenversicherung*) automatically have Long-term care Insurance. Those with private health insurance will have to apply to a private LTC insurance fund.
43. The Statutory Health Insurance Funds Association, the central representation of the statutory health and nursing care insurance funds in Germany, estimates that in 2013 over two million people were dependent on care or support because of their inability to independently cope with daily living tasks due to a physical or mental illness or disability.
44. Long-term care insured are entitled to in-patient care services when home-care or day-care is not feasible or not suitable to the individual case. The care fund will contribute to the in-patient-assistance expenditure, accordingly to the level of vulnerability of the applicant. See the SGB XI, § 42, 43.
45. SGB XI, §36–43.
46. SBG XI, §38.
47. See details in MDS (2013), pag. 73—section E "Feststellung von Personen mit erheblich eingeschränkter Alltagskompetenz", as well as in SGB XI (§ 45a).
48. As for the basic tasks, we assume the following: bathing and dental care are performed twice a day; bathing is aggregated with showering (assumed a time requirement of 20 minutes) and occurs once a week; defecation and urination (and their connected tasks) occur four times a day; three meals are consumed per day (taking 17 minutes each); getting in/out of bed occurs four times a day, taking 1 minute each time.
49. Paaßen (2012).
50. Kabinettsentwurf des 5. SGB XI ÄndG. On-line resources at: http://www.pflege-deutschland.de/pflegeversicherung/gesetz/ and http://www.pflegestufe.info/
51. The scale from 0 to 3 has the following meaning: 0—Independent; 1—Mostly independent; 2—Mostly dependent; 3—Dependent.
52. Complete reviews of the Italian LTC systems can be found in Network Non Autosufficienza (NNA) (2015), Gori (2013), Da Roit and Le Bihan (2010) Ranci and Pavolini (2012), Rebba (2010), Tediosi and Gabriele (2010) and Visca et al. (2012).
53. The main regulative references for the IA are the Laws 18/1980 and 508/1988, as well as the Prime Minister's Decree 159/2013. The monetary amount refers to year 2017, as specified in the website for the National Social Insurance Agency (INPS) at https://www.inps.it/nuovoportaleinps/default.aspx?lastMenu=49663

54. Law 296/2006 established the *livelli essenziali di assistenza* in order to provide general guidelines for regional health care.
55. Bolzano is an autonomous Province in the Region of Trentino-Alto Adige.
56. See the Interministerial Decree of 26 September 2016.
57. Specifically, the "extremely severe" loss-of-autonomy profile refers to individuals whose status fits the invalidity requirements for the IA benefit, and who experience at least one adverse health-outcome out of the following list of nine outcomes: Being in a coma, or in a persistent vegetative state, or in a minimally conscious state with a Glasgow Coma Scale score lower or equal to 10; Being constantly dependent on assisted mechanical ventilation; Being affected by dementia with a Clinical Dementia Rating Scale score of 4+; Having a spinal cord injury between C0 and C5, of level A or B according to the American Spinal Injury Association (ASIA) Impairment Scale; Having an extremely severe motor impairment with a score equal or lower than 1 in the Medical Research Council scale (for each limb), or score 9+ in the Expanded Disability Status Scale, or a Stage 5 in the Modified Hoehn and Yahr scale; Suffering from severe sensory deprivation (sight and hearing); Classified within the Level 3 of the Autism Spectrum Disorder measured with the DSM-5 scale; Having a score equal or lower than 8 in the Level of Activity in Profound/Severe Mental Retardation scale; Being in a life-threatening intensive-care dependency status, 24 hours per day.
58. The FNRA fund was promoted through the Provincial Law 9/2007, then updated with the Provincial Resolution 73/2014.
59. Multi-professional team within the Social Policies Department (Untermarzoner, 2016).
60. Scala di Valutazione Integrata dei Tempi Assistenziali.
61. Regional resolution (decreto regionale) 261/2016, Regional resolution 884/2014, and Regional Law 11/2007.
62. Barthel (1965).
63. The outcome "personal toilet" is the only exception: given that this outcome comprises multiple tasks which are not linkable to SHARE (combing hair, caring for nails, shaving), we decided to assign a score of 2 (out of 5) to any SHARE individual reporting difficulties in "bathing or showering", in order to avoid over-estimating the Barthel score.
64. The schemes we present are: Progetto per l'assistenza continua alla persona non autosufficiente (PAC), Fondo Regionale per la Non Autosufficienza. The legislation is the regional law D.G.R. 370/2010; USL 8 Casentino, 2013 and Regional law 66/2008.
65. AGENAS (2014), Profili, Razzanelli, Soli, and Marini (2009).
66. JN Morris et al. (1997).

67. Pfeiffer (1975), Profili et al. (2009).
68. Colombo et al. (2011). Primary reference: Dewey and Prince (2005).
69. See the Regional resolutions DGR 33/12/2015, and DGR 63/16/2015.
70. See Profili et al. (2009) and Visca et al. (2012).
71. Regional law D.G.R. n.370, Attachment A.
72. See, e.g., the regulation of the Casentino district, at http://www.uc.casentino.toscana.it/regolamenti/disposizioni-attuative-anno-2013.pdf.
73. The most widely used benefit was the cash-benefit, l'Assegno di Cura (DGR 4135/2006), which basically supported a home-helper (*badante*). Regional Law LR 1/2008 has established the regional fund in 2008 and further developed with LR 30/2009 for a dependency status (NA). As from 2013, DGR 1338/2013, DGR 1047/2015 a more general legislation applies.
74. See the online website http://icd.regione.veneto.it/home for further details.
75. For the highest disability ICDa the income level is lifted to €60,000.
76. The SVaMA assessment includes specific interviewer guidelines as per how to perform the cognitive evaluation, e.g., the interviewer's attitude, the location, the tone of voice, the amount of time provided for answering the questions.
77. Law 36/2006 (*Ley de Dependencia*)—Act 39/2006, on the Promotion of Personal Autonomy and Care for Dependent persons.
78. The Social Care regulation in the Care Act 2014 can be reviewed online at http://www.legislation.gov.uk/ukpga/2014/23/enacted or through a statutory guidance document (including the updates and amendments to the original Act) at https://www.gov.uk/government/publications/care-act-statutory-guidance/care-and-support-statutory-guidance. An overall review of the current available services is available online on the National Health Services website at http://www.nhs.uk/Conditions/social-care-and-support-guide/Pages/what-is-social-care.aspx
79. Further details are available online at http://www.nhs.uk/Conditions/social-care-and-support-guide/Pages/direct-payments-personal-budgets.aspx
80. Available on-line at https://www.gov.uk/government/publications/care-act-statutory-guidance and discussed in SCIE (2015)
81. After April 2020, the £23,250 upper limit will be raised to £118,000, the lower limit will be raised to £17,000. A care-cap of £72,000 has been proposed and will be introduced in 2020. Further details on ongoing legislation debate are available at http://www.ageuk.org.uk/home-and-care/care-homes/social-care-funding-changes/care-cap-and-means-test-changes/

References

AGENAS. (2014). Ricognizione della normativa regionale sulla Non Autosufficienza: AGEnzia NAzionale per i Servizi sanitari regionali.

AgeUK. (2017). *Briefing: Health and care of older people in England 2017*. Retrieved from http://www.ageuk.org.uk/Documents/EN-GB/For-professionals/Research/The_Health_and_Care_of_Older_People_in_England_2016.pdf?dtrk=true

Bäcker, G. (2016). Reform of the long-term care insurance in Germany. *ESPN Flash Report, 2016/43.*

Barthel, D. (1965). Functional evaluation: The Barthel Index. *Maryland State Medical Journal, 14*, 16–65.

BMASK. (2013a). *Ein : Blick 5. Pflege. Orientierungshilfe Zum Thema Behinderungen*. (978-3-85010-315-2). Wien: Bundesministerium für Arbeit, Soziales und Konsumentenschutz. Retrieved from http://www.sozialministerium.at/site/Soziales/Menschen_mit_Behinderungen/EINBLICK.

BMASK. (2013b). *Informationen zum Pflegegeld*. (978-3-85010-315-2). Wien: Bundesministerium für Arbeit, Soziales und Konsumentenschutz. Retrieved from http://www.sozialministerium.at/site/Soziales/Pflege_und_Betreuung/Pflegegeld/.

BMG. (2015). Gesetzentwurf der Bundesregierung. Entwurf eines Zweiten Gesetzes zur Stärkung der pflegerischen Versorgung und zur Änderung weiterer Vorschriften (Zweites Pflegestärkungsgesetz—PSG II). *Bundesministerium für Gesundheit*.

Castro-Costa, E., Dewey, M., Stewart, R., Banerjee, S., Huppert, F., Mendonca-Lima, C., … Prince, M. (2007). Prevalence of depressive symptoms and syndromes in later life in ten European countries: The SHARE study. *The British Journal of Psychiatry, 191*, 393-401. doi: https://doi.org/10.1192/bjp.bp.107.036772

Colombo, F., Llena-Nozal, A., Mercier, J., & Tjadens, F. (2011). *OECD Health policy studies help wanted? Providing and paying for long-term care: Providing and paying for long-term care* (Vol. 2011): Paris, France: OECD Publishing.

Comas-Herrera, A., Pickard, L., Wittenberg, R., Malley, J., & King, D. (2010). The long-term care system for the elderly in England. *ENEPRI Research Report* (74).

Courbage, C., & Roudaut, N. (2010). On insurance for long-term care in France. *CESifo DICE Report, 8*(2), 24–28.

Da Roit, B., & Le Bihan, B. (2010). Similar and yet so different: Cash-for-care in six European countries' long-term care policies. *Milbank Quarterly, 88*(3), 286–309.

Dewey, M. E., & Prince, M. J. (2005). Mental health. In A. Börsch-Supan & H. Jürges (Eds.), *Health, ageing and retirement in Europe—First results from the Survey of Health, Ageing and Retirement in Europe* (Vol. SHARE Codebook 8). Mannheim: MEA Eigenverlag.

Dupourqué, E., Schoonveld, S., & Bushey, J. B. (2012). AGGIR, the Work of Grids. *Long-term Care News, 32*.

European Commission. (2013a). *Your social security rights in Czech Republic*. European Commission. Retrieved from http://ec.europa.eu/social/main.jsp?catId=858.

European Commission. (2013b). *Your social security rights in France*. European Commission. Retrieved from http://ec.europa.eu/social/main.jsp?catId=858.

Fernanda Gutierrez, M., Jimenez-Martin, S., Vegas Sanchez, R., & Vilaplana, C. (2010). *The Spanish long-term care system*. ENEPRI Research Report No. 88, 15 June.

Gori, C. (2013). L'assistenza agli anziani non autosufficienti in italia: Maggioli Editore.

Gori, C., & Fernandez, J.-L. (2015). *Long-term care reforms in OECD countries*. UK: Policy Press.

INAMI. (2016). La réglementation décryptée pour l'infirmier en soins à domicile.

Jiménez-Martín, S., & Prieto, C. V. (2010). A double sample selection model for unmet needs, formal care and informal caregiving hours of dependent people in Spain. *Documento de Trabajo, 2010*, 25.

Kalwitzki, T., Müller, R., Rothgang, H., Runte, R., & Unger, R. (2015). *BARMER GEK Pflegereport 2015*.

Karakaya, G. (2009). Long-term care: Regional disparities in Belgium. *Journal of Applied Economic Sciences, 4*(7).

Katz, S., Downs, T. D., Cash, H. R., & Grotz, R. C. (1970). Progress in development of the index of ADL. *The Gerontologist, 10*(1 Part 1), 20–30. https://doi.org/10.1093/geront/10.1_Part_1.20

Lawton, M. P., & Brody, E. M. (1969). Assessment of older people: Self-maintaining and instrumental activities of daily living. *The Gerontologist, 9*(3).

MDS. (2013). *Richtlinien des GKV-Spitzenverbandes zur Begutachtung von Pflegebedürftigkeit nach dem XI. Buch des Sozialgesetzbuches*. Essen: Medizinischer Dienst des Spitzenverbandes Bund der Krankenkassen (MDS).

MISSOC. (2014). *Comparative tables on social protections—XII. Long term care*. European Commission, Department of Employment, Social Affairs and Inclusion: Mutual Information System on Social protection. Retrieved from http://ec.europa.eu/social/main.jsp?catId=815&langId=en.

Morris, J., Fries, B., Steel, K., Ikegami, N., Bernabei, R., Carpenter, G., … Topinkova, E. (1997). Comprehensive clinical assessment in community setting: Applicability of the MDS-HC. *Journal of the American Geriatrics Society, 45*(8), 1017–1024.

MPSV. (2005). *Preliminary National Report on health care and long-term care in the Czech Republic*. Ministry of Labour and Social Affairs of the Czech Republic. Retrieved from http://www.mpsv.cz/files/clanky/1343/report_health_care.pdf.

MPSV. (2009). *Social services and care allowance in the Czech Republic*. Paper presented at the Social Services—A Tool for Mobilizing Workforce and Strenthening Social Cohesion, Prague. Retrieved from http://www.mpsv.cz/files/clanky/7033/leaflet_on_social_services.pdf.

NNA (Network Non Autosufficienza). (2015). L'assistenza agli anziani non autosufficienti in Italia. In N. N. N. Autosufficienza (Ed.), *5° Rapporto. Un futuro da ricostruire* (p. 188). Santarcangelo di Romagna.

OECD. (2011). *Health at a glance: OECD indicators*. Retrieved from Paris: http://dx.doi.org/10.1787/health_glance-2011-en.

Paaßen, G. (2012). *Pflegereform 2012*. Essen: Pflegestufe.info.

Peña-Longobardo, L. M., Oliva-Moreno, J., García-Armesto, S., & Hernández-Quevedo, C. (2016). The Spanish long-term care system in transition: Ten years since the 2006 Dependency Act. *Health Policy*, *120*(10), 1177–1182. https://doi.org/10.1016/j.healthpol.2016.08.012.

Pensionsversicherungsanstalt. (2009). *Gutachterfibel-Bundespflegegeld*. Wien: .Pensionsversicherungsanstalt. Retrieved from http://www.pensionsversicherung.at/.

Pfeiffer, E. (1975). A short portable mental status questionnaire for the assessment of organic brain deficit in elderly patients. *Journal of the American Geriatrics Society*, *23*(10), 433–441.

Pilotto, A., Gallina, P., Fontana, A., Sancarlo, D., Bazzano, S., Copetti, M., ... Pellegrini, F. (2013). Development and validation of a Multidimensional Prognostic Index for mortality based on a standardized multidimensional assessment schedule (MPI-SVaMA) in community-dwelling older subjects. *Journal of the American Medical Directors Association*, *14*(4), 287–292.

Profili, F., Razzanelli, M., Soli, M., & Marini, M. (2009). Il bisogno socio-sanitario degli anziani in Toscana: i risultati dello studio epidemiologico di popolazione BiSS. *Documenti dell'Agenzia Regionale di Sanità della Toscana. Disponibile presso: www. ars. toscana. it/c/document_library/get_file.*

Ranci, C., & Pavolini, E. (2012). *Reforms in long-term care policies in Europe: Investigating institutional change and social impacts*. Springer.

Rebba, V. (2010). Il long term care in Italia: l'attuale mix pubblico-privato e il possibile ruolo della assicurazioni integrative. *Politiche sanitarie*, *11*, 113–133.

Riedel, M., & Kraus, M. (2010). The Austrian long-term care system. *ENEPRI Research Report*, *69*.

Rothgang, H. (2010). Social insurance for long-term care: An evaluation of the German model. *Social Policy & Administration*, *44*(4), 436–460.

SCIE. (2015). *Eligibility determination for the Care Act 2014*. Retrieved from London: https://www.scie.org.uk/care-act-2014/assessment-and-eligibility/eligibility/.

Sermeus, W., Pirson, M., Paquay, L., Pacolet, J., Falez, F., Stordeur, S., & Leys, M. (2010). *Le financement des soins infirmiers à domicile en Belgique*. Retrieved from Bruxelles: https://kce.fgov.be/fr/le-financement-des-soins-infirmiers-%C3%A0-domicile-en-belgique.

Sowa, A. (2010). The system of long-term care in the Czech Republic. *ANCIEN project report*. Warsaw: Centre for Social and Economic Research.

Syndicat National de Gérontologie Clinique. (1994). AGGIR Guide pratique pour la codification des variables. Principaux profils des groupes iso-ressources. *La revue de Gériatrie*, (19), 249–259.

Tediosi, F., & Gabriele, S. (2010, June 15). *Long-term care in Italy*. ENEPRI Research Report No. 80.

Untermarzoner, J. (2016). *L'assegno di cura in Alto Adige: Stato attuale. Sviluppo. Prospettive*. Retrieved from Bolzano: www.afi-ipl.org.

Visca, M., Profili, F., Federico, B., Damiani, G., Francesconi, P., Fortuna, P., … Bellentani, M. D. (2012). La Ricerca AGENAS. La presa in carico degli anziani non autosufficienti. *I QUADERNI DI MONITOR*, *30*(A), 145–183.

WHO. (2002). *Towards a common language for functioning, disability and health*. Geneva: World Health Organization Retrieved from http://www.who.int/classifications/icf/en/.

Willemé, P. (2010). The long-term care system for the elderly in Belgium. *ENEPRI Research Report* (70).

CHAPTER 4

A Comparative Analysis of LTC Systems in Terms of Inclusiveness

Abstract In Chap. 4, using micro-data from SHARE (the Survey of Health Ageing and Retirement in Europe) and ELSA (the English Longitudinal Study on Ageing), we estimate the potential coverage of each specific LTC programme, disentangling the differences between countries' coverage rates in terms of population and regulation effects. More precisely, by applying each regulation on the standard population of SHARE and ELSA, we generate a set of comparable "directly adjusted" eligibility rates (i.e., the share of the standard population that would be covered by each programme). Furthermore, we perform a pair-wise comparison of programmes' inclusiveness through a counterfactual analysis (indirect adjustment), i.e., simulating the adoption of a region's regulation on another region's population.

Keywords SHARE ELSA data • Counterfactual analysis • International comparison • Standard population • Adjusted eligibility rates

The previous chapters presented the definition of "objective vulnerability" in several European countries along with the basic rules adopted at the institutional level to provide care for vulnerable people. Our taxonomy uncovered a marked heterogeneity of the main programmes of domiciliary long-term care for the different countries and regions in Europe. We hinted to the consequences of this heterogeneity for the welfare of older

A. Brugiavini et al., *Vulnerability and Long-term Care in Europe*,
https://doi.org/10.1007/978-3-319-68969-2_4

people from an economic and social perspective, while rooting our analysis on the medical definitions and the medical assessment protocols prevailing in those countries. In this chapter, we shift the focus from the medical/epidemiological debate of what constitutes a vulnerable status to the policy relevance of determining the level of LTC utilization. In particular, we address two major issues: what is the current and future public care coverage granted to older Europeans and how can we measure the level of inequality embedded in the current programmes for access to care.

First, it is useful to discuss the state of the art of the literature investigating the relationship between health conditions and care utilization. A well-established result in the literature is that the need for LTC stems from the level of vulnerability experienced by older individuals, rather than from the ageing process per se (EUROSTAT, 2015). Therefore, detailed and appropriate measures of care needs are required to perform an analysis on care utilization as well as on the level of present and future expenditures (de Meijer, Koopmanschap, d'Uva, & van Doorslaer, 2011). In this respect, objective outcomes for functional dependency, e.g., limitations in ADL and iADL, are adopted as key variables in empirical analyses based on survey data to proxy the condition of vulnerability. They are included in three distinct ways: as *counting* variables to capture the number of occurrences; or as outcome-specific *dummies* linked to the onset of single, severe limitations; or as *dummies* for the presence of any limitations among a predetermined set of outcomes (e.g., EUROSTAT, 2015; Balia and Brau, 2013; Jiménez-Martín and Prieto, 2012; de Meijer et al., 2011; Kalwij, Pasini, and Wu, 2014). In general, functional limitations are frequently found to have an important predictive power for care utilization; moreover, the probability and quantity of care is shown to lead to increases with severity in ADL indicators (e.g., Balia and Brau, 2013). However, the way in which functional vulnerability enters the existing empirical work may vary largely with the actual assessment of needs adopted in each country, as we discussed in previous chapters. For example, when ADL and iADL are included in an econometric or empirical specification in terms of the number of limitations experienced by an individual (e.g., "number of ADL lost"), it is implicitly assumed that each loss of ADL or iADL carries the same weight in determining the latent vulnerability condition. However, several programmes assign different weights to the various outcomes, or, in some cases, only specific limitations are sufficient/necessary determinants of the definition of objective vulnerability. As an alternative approach, some authors have modelled vulnerability by building synthetic indices which would let "the data speak", thereby capturing possible nonlinearities in health outcomes and, more generally, avoiding a priori structures. For example, these indexes would be derived through statistical techniques, such as the principal components analysis or ordinal regression (Bonsang, 2009; de Meijer, Bakx, van Doorslaer, & Koopmanschap, 2015; Kapteyn & Meijer, 2013) based on several dimensions of possible "health failures". Such measures constitute examples of "reflective indices", where both the weights and the behaviour of the aggregation function are defined on a pure statistical basis (Maggino & Zumbo, 2012). Cognitive ability and mental health are often included as additional determinants, by exploiting information on depressive symptoms, ability to perform numerical operations and memory tests (Bakx, Meijer, Schut, & Doorslaer, 2014; Jiménez-Martín & Prieto, 2012; Kalwij et al., 2014).

Several studies of care utilization and public LTC expenditure are based on estimates of the current trends in the prevalence of vulnerable people, while these provide very useful insights, they do not account for the differences in the institutional set-up of public LTC and how this operates at the individual level (Lafortune & Balestat, 2007; Manton et al., 2007; Colombo, 2011; De Meijer et al., 2012). A very important macro-simulation analysis has been carried out by EUROSTAT (2015) and OECD (2016), using data on public healthcare expenditure from the System of Health Accounts (SHA), ESSPROS and EU-SILC. Their approach is developed in two steps: in the first stage a projection is made of the population in need of LTC, because of the baseline population projection and disability rates; the resulting vulnerable population is then split by the type of formal care received (at home or in institutions). Finally, average expenditures are computed for both types of formal care, and then multiplied by the projected number of recipients to obtain the overall figure for public expenditure. The minimum level of vulnerability, which is assumed to trigger the utilization of care, is assumed constant across countries and years, and corresponds to having difficulties in performing at least one ADL. A few studies make use of health conditions at the individual level, to estimate vulnerability rates, but they fail to account for the prevailing legislation faced by applicants, despite recognizing the importance of these rules (Andersen & Newman, 2005; Colombo, Llena-Nozal, Mercier, & Tjadens, 2011; Comas-Herrera et al., 2006; de Meijer et al., 2011; Gori & Fernandez, 2015). While these studies provide a useful benchmark, the contribution by Colombo and Mercier (2012) is particularly relevant to us as it highlights the importance of the choice of the target population for LTC services. They argue that this enhances the progressivity of the allowances vis-à-vis the recipient's income and/or wealth, thereby giving relatively higher priority to individuals with lower resources, but also calibrating the choice of limitations to be prioritized by an LTC system, in order to give appropriate assistance to those who are more "vulnerable". Elaborating on the trade-off between cost sustainability and adequacy of the provided benefits, they observe that "on cost-control grounds, support for domestic care and help with so-called instrumental activities of daily living (iADL) [...] should not be included in a basic package [...]. In practice, however, distinguishing between personal and domestic help can provide incentives for higher assessment-of-need and can be difficult to make, especially where services are jointly provided." As a general conclusion: "maintaining flexibility to adjust benefit coverage to changing care needs is desirable on both adequacy and quality grounds". These considerations point to a more detailed analysis of the programme, including the details of the types of limitations which are included and their relative weight.

As highlighted by de Meijer et al. (2015), changes in the observed utilization rates (across countries and time) may be driven by two different drivers which cannot be easily disentangled. First, the levels of vulnerability may vary across countries because of specific epidemiologic characteristics, and across time because of the ageing process, which can, in turn, be country-specific. Second, a programme's target population, as defined by the range of vulnerability outcomes accepted for treatment, are not homogeneous across countries or regions, as highlighted in the previous chapters. As the definition of "objective vulnerability" varies across programmes, this may generate further heterogeneity in care utilization. Hence, it is necessary to take account of the individual's eligibility status so as to isolate the impact of the institutional framework in making projections. The risk is that some of the estimated trends in take-up rates and in the burden of LTC may end up being biased.

A few empirical studies have modelled institutional differences: Comas-Herrera et al. (2003, 2006), Pickard et al. (2007) and Costa-Font et al. (2008) have produced macro-simulations of LTC expenditure using population projections based on different assumptions about future mortality rates, social changes, policy options and financing scenarios, and changes in health. The authors estimate country-specific models following a three-step methodology: first, they estimate the number of future dependent older people at an aggregate level, then they estimate the amount of services they will require and finally calculate the implied total LTC expenditures. Although the focus is on the expenditure patterns, the authors highlight the importance of the definitions used to determine the dependency rates and they provide details on the assessment procedures in each country, arguing that the results may be largely affected by these criteria. In a recent paper, Meijer et al. (2015) adopt a nonlinear version of the Oaxaca–Blinder decomposition method to show that shifts in LTC use among older Dutch adults are explained by changes in how the LTC system treats disabled people rather than by shifts in the prevalence of disability. Similarly, Bakx et al. (2014) address the differences between the German legislation and the Dutch LTC system, showing that they have an important impact on formal home care utilization by older adults in these countries. The work of Jiménez-Martín and Prieto (2012) focuses the attention on formal and informal care utilization in Spain, considering nationwide eligibility rules in a micro-data analysis, by assigning to each respondent a score computed according to the current rules. Kim and Lim (2015) exploit information on eligibility in an empirical analysis on formal and informal care in South Korea.

We have provided a partial review of the existing literature on projections for LTC expenditures: these studies clearly show that it is hard to develop a comprehensive framework for describing the implementation of eligibility rules and translate these into a tractable empirical model. The difficulties are mostly due to the lack of comparable data and to the complexity of the assessment-of-need and eligibility rules protocols (Comas-Herrera et al. 2003). This chapter aims to fill this gap, by generating comparable indices of coverage for each LTC programme. The result is a measure of the share of population aged 65+ that would be eligible to home-care services offered in their own area.

In the previous chapters we described the variety prevailing in regulation both for eligibility requirements and for the construction of the weighted scales. We have shown that the eligibility rules are typical nonlinear functions of vulnerability outcomes, where both the nonlinear pattern and the weights assigned to each outcome differ greatly across programmes. We are able to link the information on LTC assessment of need and eligibility rules envisaged by the LTC programmes with micro-data from the SHARE survey and the ELSA survey, thus generating individual-specific socio-clinical profiles. In turn, these can be compared with the requirements of the law in each country, so that we obtain an observed profile matched with the prevailing rules applicable to each individual in the sample. The final results are individual-specific indexes which are estimates of the "theoretical vulnerability status" of the respondent. These are independent of the actual LTC coverage provided to the respondent by the programme of her/his country.

By aggregating these results at the country level, we obtain country-specific rates of coverage which we will call "crude coverage rates": this is the share of individuals aged 65+ who would have access to some form of in-kind/in-cash benefit, according to the prevailing minimum eligibility thresholds, in this sense they are theoretical lower bounds. The advantage is that these rates are fully comparable across countries. This outcome represents an informative and novel instrument to assess structural differences in legislation across countries: we can separate the effect of epidemiological characteristics of the population from the regulatory environment. Furthermore, we can implement a counterfactual analysis, i.e., to implement different LTC policies on the same population hence "freezing" the epidemiological composition de Meijer et al. (2015).

4.1 Data and Sample Selection

In this section, we will make use of micro-data from the SHARE survey (Survey on Health, Ageing and Retirement in Europe; Börsch-Supan, 2017) and the ELSA survey (English Longitudinal Study of Ageing; Marmot et al., 2016). These are multidisciplinary longitudinal surveys of individuals aged 50 or older and their spouses. Data were collected through a computer-assisted personal interviewing (CAPI) programme; they cover a wide variety of items, such as household composition, economic conditions, epidemiological traits and psychological and sociological characteristics. SHARE and ELSA have the same structure and design, which in turn is based on the Health and Retirement Study (HRS). We will use the most recent waves: in particular, SHARE wave 6, collected in 2015 in Austria, Germany, Sweden, Spain, Italy, France, Denmark, Greece, Switzerland, Belgium, Israel, the Czech Republic, Poland, Luxembourg, Portugal, Slovenia, Estonia and Croatia; and ELSA wave 7, whose fieldwork ran from June 2014 to end of May 2015 in England. We refer to Axel Börsch-Supan et al. (2013) and Banks, Batty, Nazroo, and Steptoe (2016) for a detailed review of the SHARE and ELSA surveys, including methodological details and sampling procedures.

4.1.1 *Socio-clinical Variables*

SHARE and ELSA provide detailed information about the physical health status of the respondent based on self-reported conditions and limitations and on objective measures. The design of the surveys guarantees full comparability by construction; however, small deviations are possible: a full validation exercise has been carried out by Chan, Kasper, Brandt, and Pezzin (2012), and the harmonized dataset is provided within the "Gateway to Global Aging".[1,2] In particular, the dataset contains a set of questions that allow us to build, for each individual, a simplified medical profile (Table 4.1) comparable with the LTC legislations of the country. Respondents are asked to report their status in performing activities of daily living,[3] which conform to the ADL and iADL taxonomies given in Katz, Downs, Cash, and Grotz (1970), Barthel (1965) and Lawton and Brody (1969). Furthermore, the surveys include ten specific questions on *mobility limitations*.[4] All these tasks are assessed on a dichotomous scale indicating a limitation (or the absence of), but no intensity is measured. Depression is covered by two different sets of variables in SHARE and ELSA, respectively: SHARE assesses a set of 12 mood- and behaviour-related conditions (pessimism, depressed mood, suicidal thoughts, guilt, trouble sleeping, loss of interest, irritability, fatigue, inability to concentrate, lack of appetite, incapacity of enjoyment, tearfulness), which are then summarized in the EURO-D scale, whose values range from 0 to 12

Table 4.1 Summary of health limitations included in assessment-of-need scales

ADL	*iADL*	*Others*
Bathing & hygiene[a]	Communication[a]	Behavioural/Cognitive impairment[a]
Dressing[a]	Shopping for groceries/ medicines[a]	Other mobility limitations[a]
Using the toilet[a]	Cooking[a]	Informal-care utilization[a]
Transferring[a]	Housekeeping[a]	Marital status/living arrangement[a]
Continence[a]	Doing laundry[b]	Advanced medications related to post-surgical conditions[b,c]
Feeding[a]	Moving outdoor[b]	Visual/hearing impairment[a]
Moving indoor[a]	Responsibility for own medications[a]	

[a]Available

[b]Not available in ELSA

[c]Not available in SHARE

depending on the number of symptoms. A EURO-D value of 4 (or higher) has been demonstrated to be associated with a clinically significant level of depression (Dewey & Prince, 2005). ELSA allows to measure depressive symptoms with the eight-item version of the Center for Epidemiologic Studies Depression Scale (CES-D), whose outcomes include symptoms of negative affect and somatic complaints experienced in the past week through a binary response to each item resulted in a total score ranging between 0 (no symptoms) and 8 (all eight symptoms). The overall number of selected outcomes constitutes the CES-D score, with a level of 3 or higher being used to denote '*caseness*' (White et al., 2016).

Both SHARE and ELSA include four questions on mental orientation and coherence: the respondent has to report the current date, month, year and day of the week; the number of correct answers is aggregated in a generated variable (*orientation*) whose values range from 0 to 4 (the higher the better). Moreover, individuals' memory status is assessed using delayed recall of a ten-word list in widespread international use. Following the recent literature (Castro-Costa et al., 2007; Verbeek-Oudijk, Woittiez, Eggink, & Putman, 2014), we define a mental impairment when one or fewer correct answers have been recorded in the orientation questions, and memory deterioration when less than three words out of ten are recalled. Finally, information is available on the activities a respondent performed in the last month (voluntary/charity work, caring/helping friend, attending courses, taking part to sport/religious/political activities), on the use of informal help (from either inside or outside the household), or of formal care from any provider, on the use of any mobility aids, and on the hearing and seeing capabilities (self-rated). In particular, visual impairment (even using visual aids) has been coded as having a "poor" or "fair" eyesight for seeing both at distance and up-close; in principle, the ELSA general question on eyesight could be used for the English population, but given that this question is missing from SHARE, we preferred a strategy which maximizes comparability. Hearing impairment (even using hearing aids) has been similarly classified as reporting a "fair" or "poor" hearing quality.

We consider a comprehensive battery of socio-clinical conditions, which constitutes the common ground for the empirical analysis. These variables exhaust the vulnerability outcomes covered by the assessment scales previously described. Table 4.1 summarizes the various dimensions, for each limitation (or group of limitations), and also the availability of a comparable individual information in the SHARE/ELSA data. As shown, we lack information on just one group of tasks, namely the limitation in self-performing advanced medications like enemas or tube/bags maintenance.

Two adjustments had to be made between SHARE wave 6 and ELSA wave 7. The iADL limitations on moving outdoors is missing from ELSA, and has been imputed from the variable "moving indoor", similarly, being limited in "doing laundry" has been derived from the variable "doing work around the house".

4.1.2 Sample Selection and Descriptive Statistics

Our sample consists of eight countries, namely, Austria, Belgium (split into Flanders and Wallonia), the Czech Republic, England, France, Germany, Italy (four regions: Trento-Bolzano, Campania, Toscana, Veneto) and Spain. Moreover, since our analysis focuses on older people, we restrict our sample to individuals aged 65 or older. We excluded observations with missing information on socio-clinical outcomes relevant to our analysis.

The resulting sample includes 22,499 individuals, descriptive statistics are presented in Table 4.2. On average, women represent 56.7 per cent of the sample and the average age is 75.1. As far as the health conditions are concerned, limitations in iADL are more frequent than in ADL: 26.5 per cent of the sample report at least one limitation in iADL while 22.9 per cent at least one ADL limitation. Indeed, iADL tasks require a more complex neuropsychological organization and a higher involvement of cultural and environmental influences, and therefore are more likely to be the first to "fail" in the vulnerability process (LaPlante, 2010). We also report the share of individuals with at least two ADL limitations and at least two iADL limitations. Other useful cases are the joint limitations indicated by one-or-more (1+) ADL *or* one-or-more (1+) iADL limitation or the case "1+" ADL *and* "1+" iADL limitations. There are some deficits that are more easily observed: limitation in dressing and in bathing are the most frequent ADL limitation, while difficulties in doing housework, cooking and moving outdoor are the most frequent iADL limitations. As for mental limitations, the prevalence of "depression" (measured with the EURO-D and CES-D thresholds) and of cognitive impairment (through the "orientation" scale) are reported.

Table 4.2 Descriptive statistics

	Standard population	*AT*	*BE*		*CZ*	*DE*	*F*	*ES*	*EN*	*IT*[b]
			FL[a]	*WAL*						
N	22499	2224	1610	1412	3101	2364	2264	3628	5360	536
Age (mean)	75.1	75.4	75.3	75.3	73.7	75.3	75.6	76	73.7	75.7
Females (in %)	56.7	56.7	56	58	58.4	56	57.4	56.7	56.5	57.5
Health conditions:										
1+ ADL (in %)	22.9	18.9	21.4	28	18.3	21.1	23	19.7	28.7	19.3
1+ iADL (in %)	26.5	29.2	28.9	36.2	25.3	23.9	26.6	30.1	26.8	23.2
2+ ADL (in %)	11.7	10.7	9.5	14	9.9	10.8	10.8	12.8	13.1	12.4
2+ iADL (in %)	17.6	18.7	17.9	22.6	14.7	15.1	16.2	20.9	20.3	15.6
1+ ADL or iADL (in %)	33.3	32.7	34.8	42	29.8	30.2	33.5	33.4	37.5	28.1
1+ ADL and iADL (in %)	16.1	15.4	15.5	22.2	13.9	14.8	16	16.5	18	14.4
Depressed (%) (above EURO-D / CES-D thresholds)	29.4	26.1	21.9	38	22.8	26	35.4	35.4	24.8	38
Cognitively impaired in % (Orientation score below 2)	1.9	1.6	1.9	1.9	1.1	1.4	2.1	3.7	1.6	1.7
Most frequent ADL (%)	D (14) B (13)	D (12) B (11)	D (11) B (13)	D (17) B (16)	D (12) B (10)	D (13) B (11)	D (15) B (10)	D (14) B (14)	D (15) B (11)	D (13) B (13)

Data: SHARE wave 6/ELSA wave 7, individuals aged 65+. *D* dressing, *B* bathing

[a]Including Bruxelles

[b]Including Trento-Bolzano, Campania, Toscana, Veneto

Relevant heterogeneities exist across countries in the prevalence of vulnerability outcomes: Figure 4.1 provides a graphical representation of ADL and iADL limitations in the set of countries considered in this book.

The first two bars from the left represent the share of the sample reporting limitations in *at least one* ADL (first bar) or iADL (second bar). Clear differences emerge from the chart: England and Wallonia have a considerably higher ratio of ADL limitations; France, Flanders and Germany also show higher percentages than Austria, Italy (ten regions) and the Czech Republic. Although the share of iADL limitations is generally higher than the ADL limitations, the difference is small in Germany and France and is reversed in England.

As discussed in Chap. 2, many LTC legislations set an eligibility threshold in order to discriminate the severely disabled from individuals who are "mildly" vulnerable. The third and the fourth bars in the left graph of Fig. 4.1 show the shares of the sample who suffer from two ADL limitations or two iADL limitations, respectively. It is worth noting that despite the large cross-country variability in the entry conditions, the cases with "2+" ADL limitations are more uniformly distributed across countries, hence confirming that it is precisely the basic eligibility that explains the variation in Europe. While in some cases eligibility for LTC is granted on the basis of a joint requirement of limitations in both ADL *and* iADL, Table 4.2 illustrates how heterogeneity remains evident when considering individuals suffering from at least one ADL *or* one iADL.

4.2 Building an Index for LTC Coverage

The eligibility status for LTC corresponds to an assessment of an "objectively vulnerable" condition. We define the "coverage rate" or potential demand for LTC as the share of people aged 65 or older who would be labelled as "objectively vulnerable" on the basis of the prevailing legislation. We describe the steps needed to build a coverage-index by applying the LC rules to the survey-data information as detailed in the country-profiles of Chap. 3, this requires some basic notation.

Let us consider a total of J countries, with j indicating a generic country, and $j = 1,\ldots, J$. Each country has a total population of N_j people, with i being a generic individual and $i = 1,\ldots, N_j$. We assume that the number of different health and social characteristics (or "outcomes") included in any LTC regulation is H, with h being a generic outcome.

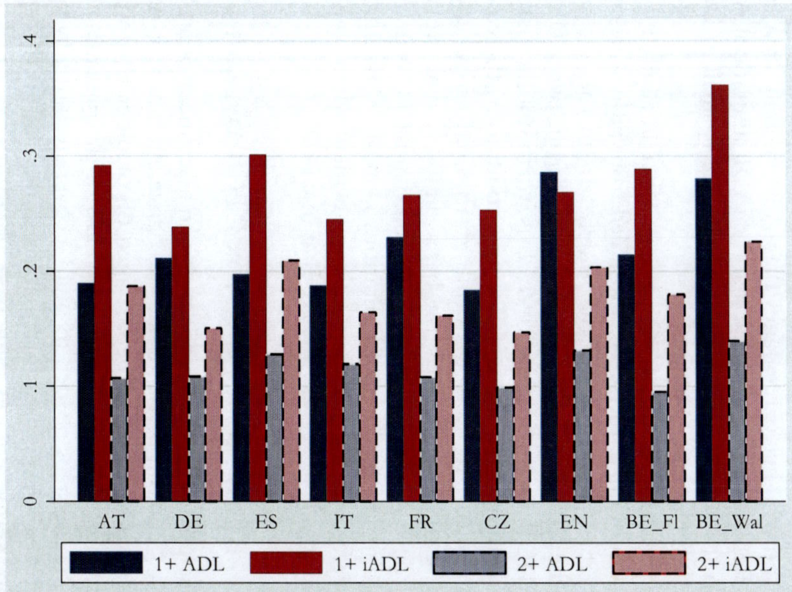

Fig. 4.1 Incidence of ADL and iADL across countries. Note: 22,499 individuals aged 65+, from SHARE wave 6 and ELSA wave 7: Austria, Belgium, the Czech Republic, England, France, Germany, Italy (four regions), Spain

We define a generic socio-clinical profile *p* characterizing an individual *i* living in country *j* as a vector $\pi_{i,j,p} = \{\alpha^1_{i,j,p},\ldots,\alpha^H_{i,j,p}\}$ where $\alpha^h_{i,j,p}$ is an indicator for the occurrence of the *h-th* socio-health outcome (assuming value 1 if it occurs, and 0 otherwise). As an example, $\pi_{i,j,5} = \{1,1,0,0,0,\ldots,0,0,0,1\}$ is a vulnerability profile (number 5, observed for individual *i* in country *j*) in which only three limitations are validated (namely the first, second and last) while the others are not present. We define as P_j the total number of different profiles existing in each country (the number is country-dependent because of country-specific epidemiologic characteristics of the population), with $p = 1,\ldots, P_j$, and $P_j \leq N_j$; the latter inequality highlights that there cannot be more observed clinical profiles than individuals in a same country, while a given profile can be shared by more than one person.[5]

Therefore, we can define $\Phi_j = \{\phi_{j,1},\ldots,\phi_{j,P_j}\}$ as the set of all possible profiles observed for the population of country *j*, where each vector $\phi_{j,p} = \{\pi_{1,j,p},\ldots,\pi_{n_{j,p},j,p}\}$ includes the information on how many individuals of country *j* share the same profile *p*, which we call $n_{j,p}$. Assuming that the profile number 5 in country *j* be shared by four individuals, than it would be $\phi_{j,5} = \{\pi_{1,j,5},\ldots,\pi_{4,j,5}\}$. Given that each individual living in *j* is assigned a socio-clinical profile, it must be $N_j = \sum_{p=1}^{P_j} n_{j,p}$, i.e., the number of individuals of *j* sharing any profile adds up to the total population of *j*.

We need to specify the following:

> ASSUMPTION 1: for a generic individual *i* with clinical profile *p* living in country *j*, the outcomes included in $\boldsymbol{\pi}_{i,j,p}$ exhaust all possible ranges of limitations included in the assessment of needs detailed in country *j*'s legislations. We will discuss the limitations implicit in this assumption later in the text.

We define with $\widetilde{\Phi}_j$ the set of socio-clinical profiles which allow the eligibility status (at any level) for any LTC programme in country *j*, that is the range of health outcomes which makes the individual potentially eligible to receive care in *j* (Andersen & Newman, 2005). The eligibility condition for an individual *i* living in country *j* can then be represented through an indicator function $I_{\widetilde{\Phi}_j}(\pi_{i,j,p})$, which takes value 1 (i.e., eligible) if the individual's profile belongs to the country's eligible profile set, that is if $\pi_{i,j,p} \in \widetilde{\Phi}_j$, and 0 otherwise.

Having computed an individual-specific eligibility indicator related to the local legislation, it is possible to define a national "crude" LTC coverage rate ω_j, as the share of people living in country j who are eligible for any programme in j:

$$\omega_j = \frac{E_j}{N_j} \tag{4.1}$$

where E_j is the eligible population, i.e., $E_j = \sum_{i=1}^{N_j} \mathrm{I}_{\tilde{\Phi}_j}\left(\pi_{i,j,p}\right)$.[6]

The indicator function **I** is a typical example of a nonlinear combinations of health indicators. As an example, the pre-2017 German national LTC programme (*Pflegeversicherung*) assessed individuals on various dimensions (items), ranging from basic/non-basic needs to cognitive limitations (Sect. 3.5.1). For each item, the legislation defines a nationwide amount of care time (in minutes), which is plausibly needed by any individual who exhibits a limitation for that item. When the assessment is complete, the sum of all the amounts of care time corresponding to the respondent's limitations is computed. The legislation would grant eligibility to all the medical profiles that present a need-of-care of at least 90 minutes per day, but with at least 45 minutes attributable to basic needs. Furthermore, the legislation includes claimants with severe cognitive limitations. In order to build the eligibility status for German older adults, we compute the overall need-of-care of each respondent in Germany, we check for the presence of severe cognitive limitations, and then apply the eligibility rule.

4.2.1 Direct Adjustment and Indirect Adjustment

The "crude coverage rates" as per equation (4.1) are not directly comparable across countries, since they embed a "regulation effect" and a "population effect", which cannot be disentangled at this stage. Particularly in the case of cross-sectional samples, where we cannot fully explain the sources of heterogeneity due, for example, to cohort effects, we would estimate higher shares of eligible individuals in one country either because its LTC system is on average more inclusive (this is captured by the country-specific eligibility function f), or because its population has worse health-conditions (i.e., the distribution of observed socio-clinical profiles is country-specific), or both (de Meijer et al., 2015).

To allow for international comparability, we adopt a "direct adjustment" or standardization, which has been widely used in the health economics literature (see, e.g., Gravelle (2003), Schokkaert and Van de Voorde (2009)), and it resembles the Oaxaca—Blinder decomposition approach (de Meijer et al., 2015). In particular, in order to compare the coverage rates of country A versus country B, the direct-adjustment methodology requires to apply, separately, the LTC rules of the two countries to a standard population (e.g., the population of A plus the population of B). The overall number of individuals eligible under each set of rules should then be expressed as a ratio over the total standard population. The directly adjusted rates are comparable relative measures of coverage: given a set of J countries whose overall population (hereafter, "standard") is $N = \sum_{j=1}^{J} N_j$, the *directly adjusted coverage rates* ω_j^D of the LTC legislations implemented by country j is defined as:

$$\omega_j^D = \frac{E_j^D}{N} \tag{4.2}$$

The numerator, $E_j^D = \sum_{j=1}^{J}\sum_{i=1}^{N_j} \mathrm{I}_{\tilde{\Phi}_j}\left(\pi_{i,j,p}\right)$ represents the eligible individuals (in accordance with the rules of country j) out of the total standard population. Moreover, by repeating this procedure for each LTC regime, we can derive programme-specific directly-adjusted coverage rates.

An alternative approach, known as *indirect adjustment*, requires performing pair-wise counterfactual analysis as follows: (i) apply the LTC eligibility rules of a country s on the population of a different country, say j, with $s \neq j$, thus obtaining an *expected* number of eligible individuals belonging to the population of j; (ii) compare this result with the number of individuals living in j that are eligible under the local legislations (the *observed* eligible population E_j). In particular, by defining the *expected* (counterfactual) eligible population with $E_{j,s} = \sum_{i=1}^{N_j} \mathrm{I}_{\tilde{\Phi}_s}\left(\pi_{i,j,p}\right)$, the *indirectly-adjusted coverage rate* $\chi_{j,s}$ can be defined as:

$$\chi_{j,s} = \frac{E_{j,s}}{E_j} - 1 \tag{4.3}$$

Whenever $\chi_{j,s}$ is greater (lower) than zero when the eligibility rules of country *s* are more (less) inclusive than those of country *j*, both applied to the population of *j*.

The methodology described above delivers extremely valuable information on the comparative generosity of LTC systems; however, there exist potential sources of measurement error which have to be discussed. A first, minor concern is that we focus on main national/regional care programmes, while it must be recalled that these national LTC are often complemented by additional care programmes at the community level, which may be based on different rules. It is obvious that in the type of application we present in this book and given the variety of rules observed at the macro level, it would be impossible to consider other LTC provisions which may entail to gather information at the municipality level. Turning the attention to aspects of the application which may have an impact on the results, we pointed out in Chap. 3 that an important issue is the matching procedure of the actual legislation with the micro-data available in the surveys. In fact, the characteristics under investigation in the assessment-of-need for LTC do not always match exactly the information provided by the dataset. Apart from a few cases, when there is no valuable information in the data which would allow us to complete a valid match, in general the discrepancy is due to cases of functional limitations which are recorded dichotomously (0 or 1) in the ELSA/SHARE data, while the legislation entails an intensity score. In these cases, we could not tease out from the data the *degree* of the potential loss of autonomy, but simply assign the presence/absence of the limitation. Another potential source of discrepancy is due to the way health information is collected in the dataset as it is mostly self-reported, while in the actual assessment-of-needs a medical doctor or a nurse may carry out the medical test. There exists a risk that the survey-based eligibility rates are biased. They are underestimates, e.g., if respondents do not report limitation conditions that would be categorized as such by a trained evaluator, or, at the other extreme, limitations are overestimates, e.g., if the respondent reports difficulties which are relevant for the individual herself/himself but that would be regarded as "mild" by the legislation and thus would not require provision of care (EUROSTAT, 2015). However, the interviewers who are in charge of the *face-to-face* CAPI interview are highly qualified professionals trained to signal unreliable answers, so that by and large the reported limitations are correct. The quality of the data has been confirmed by the validation exercise carried out for ADL or iADL limitations[7]. Hence, there should be no systematic bias in these estimates as, on average, we should obtain a fair representation of vulnerability. A more serious concern is that, if the legislation envisages some means-testing, our methodology would face problems in matching the rule with the income/wealth levels reported in the dataset. In fact, the items normally used in the legislation are complex combinations of different income sources which do not find an easy counterpart. Although means-testing is contemplated only by a few programmes, comparability is partly jeopardized by this shortcoming. Finally, although the legislation may entail clear assessment and eligibility 'objective' rules, some discretion remains with the multidisciplinary team performing the assessment of the applicant. In our exercise, we are assuming that the laws and the guidelines are carefully implemented by the local evaluators or that deviations from the norm occur randomly across countries and programmes: this is a potential discrepancy which is beyond our control, but once again there should be no systemic bias coming from these possible deviations.

4.3 Results

4.3.1 Crude Rates of LTC Coverage in Europe

Table 4.3 presents the results on *crude rates* of eligibility for people aged 65 and over in selected countries. The prevailing legislation refers to the year 2015 and the datasets are the sixth wave of SHARE and the seventh wave of ELSA. We do not include rates for the Italian regions, since the sample size at the regional level is too small to generate sensible estimates. In order to provide some comparability with official statistics, we also compute the crude rates using the set of rules of the year 2010 and 2013, using the fourth and the fifth waves of SHARE.[8] As already detailed, crude rates represent the share of 65+ individuals that would be defined as eligible to care (i.e., being "objectively vulnerable") according to the country rules where they reside. Results for France and Belgium are the results of applying multiple programmes and averaging over regions, particularly for Belgium.

Table 4.3 Crude LTC eligibility rates (% of 65+ population), different years

	Rules in 2015 (SHARE w6, ELSA w7) (%)	*Rules in 2013 (SHARE w5)*	*Rules in 2010 (SHARE w4)*
Austria	12	13.1	13.5
Belgium	8.2	8.8	9.6
Belgian APA	*7.3*	*7.8*	*8.6*
Belgian INAMI	*5.1*	*5.6*	*6.3*
Belgian Flemish insurance[a]	*3.9*	*5*	*4.2*
Czech Republic	12.2	11.9	10.6
England	15.9	Not applicable	Not applicable
France	14	13.2	13.4
French APA	*10.4*	*9.2*	*9.5*
French AM	3.6	*3.9*	*3.9*
Germany	11.7	11.7	12
Spain	16	15.4	15.3

Data: share of individuals aged 65 or more, data from SHARE wave 6, 5, 4 and ELSA wave 7.

Means-tested not implemented

[a]Coverage for the Belgian Flemish Insurance is based on Flemish population only

Crude rates provide an estimate of potential demand for care (in our case a lower bound), so that predicted "eligibility" does correspond to the actual take-up of LTC benefit. Furthermore, SHARE does not include information on whether the respondent filed an application for LTC benefits, so that we can compare the "theoretical eligibility" estimated by our procedure and the actual take up, but we cannot say about pending situations.[9] Also, it should be mentioned that in interpreting the results of Table 4.3 one has to be cautious that we are not evaluating the entire social care package of a country, but rather we focus on provisions for a target population potentially requiring home care.

The estimated rates vary substantially across countries: the share of eligible individuals is higher in England, Spain and France, with average rates between 16 per cent and 13 per cent. The French rates are obtained as the sum of the APA and *Aide Menagere* eligibility rates: roughly two-thirds of the France rate is due to the APA programme (around 10 per cent). The German rates are always computed according to the pre-2017 legislations and lie slightly below 12 per cent level. The Austrian rates are based on either the threshold of 60 hours per month (for 2013 and 2015), or 50 hours per month (for 2009–2010), and reach an average rate of about 13 per cent overall. Crude rates for the Czech Republic range between 10.5 per cent and 12 per cent, while those for Belgium (averaging Flanders and Wallonia) suggest that 8–9.5 per cent of the sample is eligible to any of the three programmes (or either of the two, in Wallonia). Among these, the Belgian APA has the highest eligibility rate (around 8 per cent), followed by the national home-care (INAMI/RIZIV) at 5–6 per cent and the Flemish LTC Insurance (4–5 per cent of the sole Flemish sample).

How do these numbers compare to the actual take-up of LTC in the different countries? While this is a very interesting policy issue that we can discuss with our data, we have to be cautious in the way the comparison is interpreted. First, our coverage rates focus on the programme-specific definition of "objective vulnerability", which is essentially a proxy for need-of-care based on a combination of functional and cognitive characteristics. Yet official statistics do not report evidence on the "need-of-care", which is not directly observable, but rather on the use of care and care benefits (Willemé, 2010), in the form of an ex post measure of observed access to care. Second, as discussed in the introduction to this chapter, results may be driven by other determinants besides the eligibility condition. In this respect, it is useful to recall that LTC services may be attributed to the health budget in some countries and to the social care budget in others (Costa-Font, Courbage, & Swartz, 2015; OECD, 2016; Pickard et al., 2007). Third, since we do not categorize individuals by the intensity of their objective vulnerability status, our eligible population is likely to include people actually enrolled in nursing homes, and who do not show up in the records on home-care programmes utilization. Fourth, we do not account for means-testing in computing our coverage rates.

The comparison with official records show that our estimates are reliable. The official records for Austria (BMASK, 2011; OECD, 2011; Riedel & Kraus, 2010) show that, on average, the observed coverage of the national LTC programme lies around 15 per cent for the 65+ population in the early 2010s, thus matching closely our results. Our estimates for Belgium match the figures provided by Karakaya (2009), who implement the same set of rules for the same three programmes on administrative data and obtain similar results: prevalence rates are around 9 per cent in 2010. Data on the actual utilization of home care report a coverage of 6.5% in the years 2006–2010 (Gerkens & Merkur, 2010), which is in line with our estimates. We get similar results for Germany where take-up rates are around 11 per cent of the population aged 65 or more (Schultz, 2010); the percentage is as high as 13 per cent in more recent years (Statistisches

Bundesamt, 2015). Our estimated coverage for England is around 15 per cent for people 65 and older in the ELSA survey. Although such result reflects the high prevalence of functional limitations in England, as shown in Fig. 4.1 (the highest incidence of people having 1 or 2 ADL among the selected countries), the rate is substantially higher than reported in comparable data for the year 2015 (about 6.5 per cent) (AgeUK, 2017). Such a discrepancy can be explained by both the application of means-testing and the "discouraged older adults" effect: AgeUK reports about one million people aged 65+ did not receive the help they needed, accounting for 12 per cent of the older eligible people. In France, recent statistics show that around 11.5 per cent of the 65+ population had access to the APA between 2010 and 2014, which is close to our predicted coverage, whereas the remaining programmes for Help to Older Individuals (*Aides aux personnes agees*) covered an additional 2 per cent of the same population, bringing the total coverage to around 14 per cent (Borderies, Amar, & Leroux, 2016). In this respect, our figures, which assign a coverage between 3 and 4 per cent to the non-APA programmes, seem to slightly overestimate the actual beneficiaries of complementary assistance. With regard to the Spanish system, the new legislations have been progressively implemented since 2007, generating situations of "dependency limbo", i.e., individuals officially assessed as entitled to benefits who have not actually received any provision. The share of 65+ individuals favourably evaluated for LTC benefits (not necessarily receiving it) is around 15 per cent in 2015s (Peña-Longobardo, Oliva-Moreno, García-Armesto, & Hernández-Quevedo, 2016), thus matching closely our score.

4.3.2 Results of the Direct Adjustment Methodology

As discussed in Sect. 4.2.1, crude rates cannot be used to compare inclusiveness of the different programmes because they do not allow to disentangle the "regulation effect" from the "population effect". Figure 4.1 makes clear that there is significant heterogeneity in vulnerability rates across countries in our dataset. To overcome this problem, we compute directly-adjusted eligibility rates based on the standard population described in Table 4.2 and show the results in Table 4.4 and in Figure 4.2. For France and Belgium, we report the rates both at the level of the programme and at the level of the country. Given the "counterfactual" nature of the direct-adjustment analysis, we can also evaluate the coverage rates of programmes that were not actually implemented at the time of data

Table 4.4 Directly-adjusted inclusiveness rates

	Directly-adjusted inclusiveness rate (%)	*95% Confidence interval (%)*	
AT <2010	14.3	13.6	14.9
AT <2016	12.4	11.7	13.0
AT 2016	11.8	11.2	12.4
BE-FL	8.2	7.7	8.7
BE-W	7.6	7.1	8.1
be, apa	6.8	6.3	7.2
be, inami	5.7	5.3	6.1
be-fl, bel	4.9	4.5	5.3
CZ	13.7	13.1	14.4
DE 2017	11.4	10.8	12.0
DE<2017	12.2	11.6	12.9
EN	15.3	14.7	16.0
ES	12.9	12.2	13.5
FR	15.1	14.5	15.8
fr - am	3.5	3.1	3.8
fr - apa	11.6	11.0	12.3
IT-Bolzano	13.2	12.7	14.0
IT-Campania	2.1	1.8	2.4
IT-Toscana	5.6	5.3	6.2
IT-Veneto	7.8	7.3	8.3

Note: 22,499 individuals aged 65+, from SHARE wave 6 and ELSA wave 7: Austria, Belgium, Czech Republic, England, France, Germany, Italy (four regions) Spain

collection, i.e., the rule in place in 2010 and 2016 in Austria and the rules implemented in Germany. We also provide coverage estimates for the four Italian programmes described in Sect. 3.6.

The adjusted rates of coverage highlight the existing heterogeneity in eligibility rates due to the definition of need-of-care. The very concept of "objective vulnerability" prevailing in each country, as discussed in Sect. 2.2 and detailed in Chap. 3, generates wide variability of potential coverage. The English and the French programmes entail rates above 15 per cent, while in Austria and in the Czech Republic adjusted rates are around 14 per cent%. Several programmes, namely the Italian case in Bolzano, the Spanish programme, the German system (pre-2017) and the Austrian system, imply rates between 12 and 13 per cent while the current German rules imply an eligibility coverage of 11.4 per cent. The two Belgian regions, along with the Veneto region, cover roughly 8 per cent of our standard sample, in Toscana the rate is 5.8 per cent and in Campania is 2.1

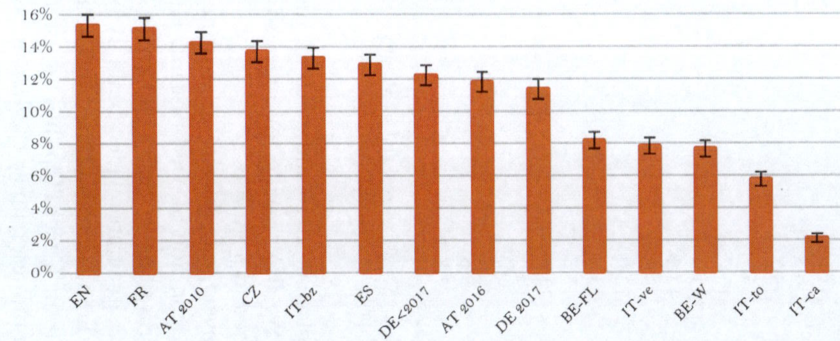

Fig. 4.2 Directly-adjusted eligibility rates (SHARE wave 6, ELSA wave 7). Note: 22,499 individuals aged 65+, from SHARE wave 6 and ELSA wave 7: Austria, Belgium, Czech Republic, England, France, Germany, Italy (four regions) Spain. Confidence intervals (95%) are shown

per cent. It is interesting to note how the population-adjustment produces some important reversals in ranking when comparing with the crude rates of Table 4.3. On the one hand, the English definition of LTC produces the highest coverage levels (15.3 per cent) even after the adjustment, while, on the other hand, the Spanish and Walloon rules generate lower rates (12.9 per cent and 7.6 per cent, respectively) than in the crude case (16% and 9.7%). At the other extreme, the potential demand for the Czech, Flemish and German samples are higher than for the case of crude-rates.

A qualitative analysis of our results shows that eligibility rules which directly account for iADL (alongside ADL) have higher coverage rates. Similarly, higher inclusiveness is generated by assessment strategies which evaluate the vulnerability status through the accumulation of functional deficits or through the presence of cognitive limitations. Conversely, programmes focused on ADL-only (or perhaps a subset of them), or requiring the joint presence of functional, behavioural and cognitive problems in order to trigger a potential demand for care.

It is useful to provide a deeper insight into the mechanisms producing these results.

The assessment of need introduced with the *English* Care Act of 2014 focuses on a wide range of ADL and iADL. At first, the list of limitations looks fairly narrow, as it is often the case that ADL or iADL are used within bundles. E.g., the "nutrition" and the "personal hygiene" segments, including both one ADL (eating food, bathing self) and one iADL (preparing the food, laundering clothes). However, in addition to functional deficits, the programme includes social exclusion, social role and childcaring responsibilities, which expands the role of LTC. A minimum threshold of having difficulties in two or more outcomes is set: this low threshold, along with the absence of a clear hierarchy in the assessment scale, generates relatively high coverage rates.

The *French* system tackles vulnerability conditions according to a double-target design: the two programmes, *Aide Menagere* (3.5 per cent), and APA (11.6 per cent), display very different estimated potential demand. This is unsurprising, given that the former is a "residual" programme aimed at delivering assistance for "mild" iADL conditions of vulnerability (mostly individuals with difficulties in shopping for groceries, in cooking or in hygiene tasks), which are not severe enough to get access to the latter (which requires—roughly—the loss of two ADL or the presence of mental/cognitive disorders). Even though this "combo" covers a relatively high (and heterogeneous) share of population, the contributions supplied through the *Aide Menagere* are small.

Legislations in *Austria and Germany (pre-2017)* share several features in their assessments-of-need protocols, and yet differences emerged in their eligibility rules. The Austrian regulation requires individuals to report a need-of-care corresponding to a fixed amount of hours per month, emerging from ADL, iADL and cognitive/mental difficulties. The minimum monthly threshold increased in, roughly, seven years, from 50 to 60 to 65 hours. The pre-2017 German LTC Insurance sets a minimum eligibility threshold in terms of two requirements: an individual should need at least 45 minutes per day (22.5 hours per month) for help with ADL, and an overall amount of 90 minutes per day (45 hours per month) for both ADL and iADL. The German system places more emphasis on ADL limitations, as it requires a specific minimum requirement of 45 minutes per day. On the other hand, the German programme granted eligibility to cognitively impaired individuals, while the Austrian regulation accounts for such impairments by adding 25 hours of need-of-care to the overall amount. As a result, the difference between the rates of these national programmes is moderate: the Austrian system (in its 50 hours version) delivers a 2 per cent higher coverage than the German one (14.2 per cent vs 12.2 per cent). The current vulnerability assessment in *Germany (since 2017)* generates a potential demand which is only slightly lower than in the pre-reform framework. Less weight is given to mobility and functionality (which account to roughly 50 per cent of the total score), with cognitive, behavioural and psychological outcomes accounting up to 15 per cent, therapy-related requirements to 20 per cent, and capability of planning for everyday life to 15 per cent.

The four *Italian* regional LTC programmes exhibit extremely heterogeneous potential coverage rates, stemming from the striking different definitions of "objective vulnerability" they adopt. The province of *Bolzano* shares common traits with the Austrian programme, in that it assigns different time amounts for functional (ADL and iADL), cognitive and behavioural limitations. Its eligibility threshold amounts to 56 hours per month, thus making it slightly less (more) inclusive than the 2010 (2016) Austrian rules. The *Veneto region* adopts rules based on a wide multidimensional assessment scale (SVaMA), encompassing several vulnerability limitations which do not including iADL while accounting for the informal care availability (carer-sighted) and for an overall "need for medical assistance". The fixed threshold of 10+ points requires individuals to present some limitations in most of the vulnerability dimensions to get access to care. Thus, the reduced coverage rate of 7.8 per cent. The definition of "need-of-care" in *Toscana* follows similar mechanisms, in that it encompasses functional (no iADL), cognitive and behavioural outcomes. The eligibility requirements are slightly higher than in Veneto, since at least moderate issues should be present in all three of the evaluated dimensions, thus the lower coverage rate of 5.8 per cent. Finally, *Campania*'s LTC assistance is targeted to individuals having severe loss-of-autonomy. Although the multidimensional SVaMA scale is adopted to build an individual's clinical profile, eligibility is granted on the basis of the sole functional (Barthel) component of the scale, which excludes iADL. The implemented threshold (55+) identifies severe dependency conditions, thus reducing the potential demand to 2.1 per cent of our standard sample.

Directly-adjusted eligibility rates computed on the standard population for the *Spanish* programme are sensibly lower than the correspondent crude rates presented in the previous Section, driven by the relatively higher prevalence of, especially, iADL limitations in the country's sample population. The definition of vulnerability embedded in the Spanish system encompasses mostly functional (both ADL and iADL, with a substantial weight of 34 per cent given to mobility-related tasks) and cognitive outcomes, similarly to the Czech Republic and the pre-2017 German legislations. Indeed, the selected minimum eligibility threshold (25 out of 100) leads to a coverage rate which is similar to the two above programmes.

In Belgium, older adults have access to different kinds of programmes, depending on the region in which they live. Two nationwide programmes of care are evaluated: the home assistance in-kind provided by the National Institute for Sickness and Disability Insurance and the APA. The former has a degree of inclusiveness of 5.7 per cent. Such a rate is rather high when compared to all the other programmes, when one considers that the INAMI is the only one which targets specific limitations. Indeed, although the basis for the need assessment are ADL limitations and cognitive deficits, limitations in bathing and dressing are necessary to trigger eligibility. Since these limitations are those with the highest frequency of occurrence in our sample (Table 4.2), the programme still reaches 5.7 per cent of individuals. On the other hand, the Belgian APA has a more extensive assessment-of-need scale, yet its eligibility rules set a higher minimum vulnerability level so that its inclusiveness rate is estimated at just a percentage point higher (6.8 per cent). The overall inclusiveness rate for the public LTC system in Wallonia (7.6 per cent) represents the share of individuals who are eligible for *at least one* of the aforementioned programmes. In the Flemish region (as well as in Bruxelles), older adults are offered a supplementary allowance (the assessment of need is performed through the so-called BEL scale), which targets individuals with a substantial vulnerability status defined by the accumulation of ADL, iADL and mental/cognitive limitations. This supplementary programme has a coverage degree of 4.9 per cent; it is worth noticing that 0.6 per cent of the sample[10] is eligible to the specific Flemish programme, but not to the remaining two: thus, the overall eligibility rate for Flanders is higher (8.2 per cent) than for Wallonia (7.6 per cent).[11]

In discussing these comparisons, it is crucial to point out how each definition of vulnerability identifies a very specific eligible "target population": even when two programmes end up with identical coverage rates, there may be differences between the actual individuals who are eligible for the two programmes. This discrepancy is driven by the inclusion/exclusion of specific outcomes in the assessment of need and by the different weighting of the single outcomes in determining the eligibility status. In Fig. 4.3, we select four pairs of programmes with similar eligibility rates and report the share of the standard population who would be eligible to both, or to just one of them. Panel (a) shows that, although the overall eligibility rate for the reformed German programme is slightly lower than the pre-reform one, 2.5 per cent of the standard population would be eligible for the former, yet not for the latter; indeed, the share of individuals eligible to both programmes amounts to just 8.9 per cent. Similarly, Flanders' and Veneto's LTC rules both cover 6 per cent of the population, yet the former covers an additional 2.2 per cent which are not "objectively vulnerable" under Veneto's rules, which, in turn, exclusively covers an additional 1.8 per cent. The same happens for programmes with high overall coverage, as the English one (15.3 per cent) and the French one (15.1 per cent), or the Czech one (13.7 per cent) or that in Bolzano (13.3 per cent): results show that more than only 2 per cent of the sample is eligible for one of them.

4.3.3 *Results on Coverage Rates from the Indirect Adjustment*

The analysis in the previous section provided comparable estimates of regulation's inclusiveness by adopting a "European" standard population. It

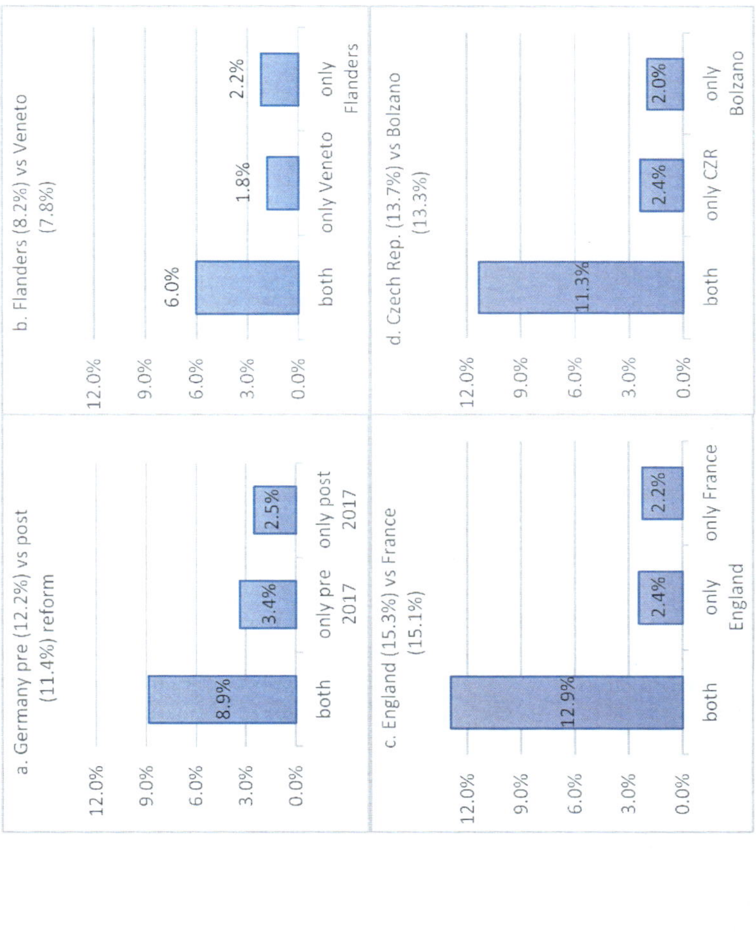

Fig. 4.3 Comparison of programme-specific eligible populations (in % of standard population). Note: 22,499 individuals aged 65+, from SHARE wave 6 and ELSA wave 7: Austria, Belgium, the Czech Republic, England, France, Germany, Italy (four regions) Spain

Table 4.5 Percentage change in national eligibility rates when applying alternative regimes

Country	*Alternative regimes*							
	Austrian (2016) (%)	*Flemish*	*Czech (%)*	*German (2017) (%)*	*English (%)*	*Spanish (%)*	*French (%)*	*Italy-Bolzano (%)*
AT		−22.4	**+20.3**	−6.2	**+25.1**	**+0.5**	**+19.4**	**+2.9**
BE_Fl	**+56.2**	–	**+84.9**	**+25.9**	**+105.8**	**+73.5**	**+127.9**	**+80.7**
CZ	−14.9	−40.4	–	−25.1	**+12.2**	−8.7	**+5.3**	-9.7%
DE	**+8.8**	−29.3	**+20.4**	–	**+36.4**	**+14.4**	**+31.0**	**+18.0**
EN	−22.5	−51.8	−12.5	−30.1	–	−20.7	**+2.8**	-16.7
ES	−9.6	−26.8	**+4.1**	−9.6	**+5.0**	–	**+5.4**	**+2.9**
FR	−28.1	−50.5	−7.2	−26.4	**+10.7**	−14.0	–	-15.7

Note: 23,587 individuals aged 65+, from SHARE wave 6 and ELSA wave 7: Austria, Belgium, Czech Republic, England, France, Germany, Spain

is also useful to perform the mirror exercise and to perform pair-wise comparisons to focus on specific characteristics of the population and generate counterfactuals. In particular, we implement different definitions of vulnerability on the same "population" of a specific country/region, thus obtaining counterfactual eligibility rates; we then compare such rates with those obtained under the original national rules (the crude rates). The basic question is "How much would the LTC coverage rates in country X change under the rules of country Y ?" Table 4.5 reports the percentage changes in eligibility rates when applying each set of rules. The change is indicated by "alternative regime", this is performed for each sample listed under the column "country", and compared it with the crude eligibility rates. For Austria and Germany, we adopt the most recent rules (i.e., 2016 for Austria and 2017 for Germany). E.g., when applying the Czech Republic's definition of objective vulnerability on the Austrian population, the resulting eligibility rates increase the number of eligible older individuals by 20.3% with respect to the original Austrian 2016 definition [the corresponding analytical formulation is described in equation (4.3)].

Table 4.5 may be read row-wise as well as column-wise. When looking at the rows, the application keeps fixed the population of the country (the sample) in order to evaluate how each alternative LTC regulation would affect eligibility rates. When looking at the columns, the application fixes a "treatment", i.e., an LTC regime, and it assess the impact of different legislations on different samples.

Results from this analysis are in line with what obtained in the direct adjustment case, but they provide a clear indication on how much a given set of rules would alter the current eligibility coverage in each country. The Flemish definition of LTC is more conservative than any other programme: it would reduce the eligibility rates substantially (as much as a 50 per cent reduction) if applied to the French or English population. At the other extreme, when applying the French rules and the English rules—which normally deliver the highest coverage rates—one would see an increase in the potential demand for care of all countries. The change is higher for countries where the system is tight to start with (see, e.g., the magnitude of the rates for Flanders). Our results provide a very useful interpretation of the European systems: different approaches to LTC tend to target different groups of the population and tend to be more (less) selective in their coverage policies.

Finally, we can isolate the "population effect", i.e. the epidemiologic characteristics of the population, and how these interact with the legislation. Figure 4.4 provides a graphical representation of the indirect-adjustment rates for three selected LTC cases (the Czech, the Spanish and

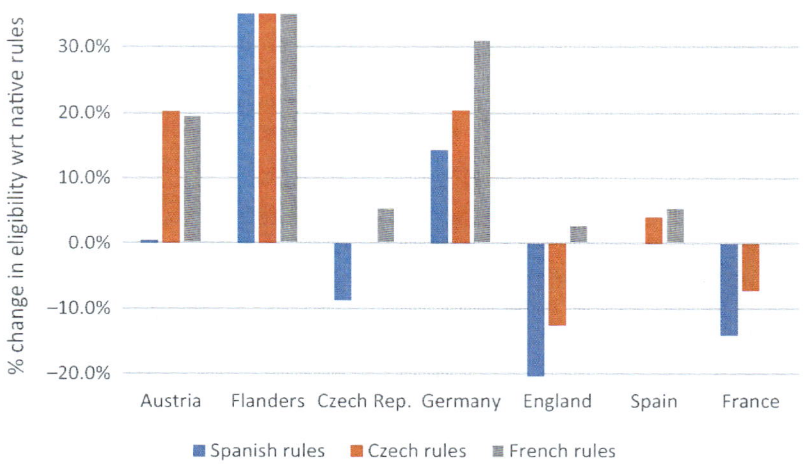

Fig. 4.4 % change in eligibility rules for applying Czech, Spanish or French definitions of eligibility. Note: 22,499 individuals aged 65+, from SHARE wave 6 and ELSA wave 7: Austria, Belgium, Czech Republic, England, France, Germany, Spain

the French systems) on each of the seven country-samples considered. The point is that a set of rules may be more inclusive on paper, but the impact on eligibility rates depends on actual population characteristics. We have seen how the implementation of the English regime leads, on average, to the highest increases in coverage, but in Belgium-Flanders the impact is lower than elsewhere. Similarly, the French regime, very close to the English one in terms of inclusiveness, when applied to Austria would lead to a lower coverage increase than would the Czech rules. Furthermore, programmes may have a similar impact on some people and not on others: the Czech system, the Spanish system and the programme in Bolzano would entail an increase in coverage rates of around 15–20 per cent if applied to Germany, while the effect on the Austrian population ranges from +20 per cent to 0–3 per cent.

Notes

1. https://g2aging.org
2. All the SHARE questions are worded in order to be comparable across countries.
3. Thirteen tasks are included in all the SHARE and ELSA waves: (i) dressing, including putting on shoes and socks; (ii) walking across a room; (iii) bathing or showering; (iv) eating, such as cutting up one's food; (v) getting in and out of bed; (vi) using the toilet, including getting up and down; (vii) using a map to determine how to get around in a strange place; (vii) preparing a hot meal; (ix) shopping or buying groceries; (x) making telephone calls; (xi) taking medicines, following medical prescriptions; (xii) doing work around the house or garden; and (xiii) managing money, such as paying bills and keeping track of expenses. SHARE wave 6 includes also: (xiv) Leaving the house independently and accessing transportation services; (xv) Doing personal laundry. An additional question covers the dependency over urinary incontinence, or the involuntary loss of urine, in all of the ELSA waves as well as in SHARE waves 1–4, while the item is missing from wave 5, and included in wave 6 through a question about the use of incontinence pads. ELSA includes a question on faecal incontinence, as well as on two further tasks as "Recognising when you are in physical danger" and "Communication (speech, hearing or eyesight)".
4. The tasks covered are: (i) walking 100 meters (yards in ELSA); (ii) sitting for about two hours; (iii) getting up from a chair after sitting for long periods; (iv) climbing several flights of stairs without resting; (v) climbing one flight of stairs without resting; (vi) stooping, kneeling, or crouching; (vii) reaching or extending your arms above shoulder level; (viii) pulling or

pushing large objects like a living room chair; (ix) lifting or carrying weights over 10 pounds/5 kilos, like a heavy bag of groceries 10; (x) picking up a small coin from a table.

5. If $P_j = N_j$ then $n_{p,j} = 1$ for every p.
6. Although this crude rate is computed for all the LTC programmes implemented in a country, programme-specific coverage-rates can be calculated in a similar way.
7. Similar concerns are expressed by Bonsang (2009) and Balia and Brau (2013). Reliability of self-reported health-conditions is investigated in Bound (1991), Baker, Stabile, and Deri (2004), Dwyer and Mitchell (1999), LaPlante (2010). A cross-survey comparison between HRS, SHARE and ELSA is performed in Chan et al. (2012).
8. We cannot use estimate crude rates for the England LTC legislation before 2015, since the reviewed eligibility rules were not yet implemented.
9. As discussed in Carrino and Orso (2015), there are situations of failure in take-up (i.e., individuals who do not make use of formal home-care while being eligible) or excessive take-up (i.e., individuals who report receiving care, despite failing eligibility). There are at least two reasons, besides measurement error, for observing this pattern: first, formal-care, as it is asked in SHARE, includes privately-paid care not publicly provided. Second, the eligibility index is based on main home-care programmes regulated at national or regional level, yet not also on municipal-level, since the exact municipality of residence is not available in SHARE due to non-disclosure policies.
10. The difference between the inclusiveness rates for Flanders and Wallonia.
11. From a resources-oriented perspective, receiving an additional allowance from the Flemish government can affect individual behaviour. Our interest is to look at whether individuals are covered under a specific regime in the *status quo*.

References

AgeUK. (2017). In AgeUK (Ed.), *Briefing: Health and care of older people in England 2017*. UK: AgeUK.

Andersen, R., & Newman, J. F. (2005). Societal and individual determinants of medical care utilization in the United States. *Milbank Quarterly, 83*(4), Online-only. https://doi.org/10.1111/j.1468-0009.2005.00428.x

Baker, M., Stabile, M., & Deri, C. (2004). What do self-reported, objective, measures of health measure? *Journal of Human Resources*, *39*(4), 1067–1093. https://doi.org/10.2307/3559039

Bakx, P., Meijer, C., Schut, F., & Doorslaer, E. (2014). Going formal or informal, who cares? The influence of public long-term care insurance. *Health Economics*, *24*, 631–643. https://doi.org/10.1002/hec.3050

Balia, S., & Brau, R. (2013). A country for old men? Long-term home care utilization in Europe. *Health Economics*, *23*, 1185–1212. https://doi.org/10.1002/hec.2977

Banks, J., Batty, G. D., Nazroo, J., & Steptoe, A. (2016). *The dynamics of ageing: Evidence from the English Longitudinal Study of ageing 2002–15 (Wave 7)*. London: The Institute for Fiscal Studies.

Barthel, D. (1965). Functional evaluation: The Barthel index. *Maryland State Medical Journal*, *14*, 16–65.

BMASK. (2011). Österreichischer Pflegevorsorgebericht 2011. *Bundesministerium für Arbeit, Soziales und Konsumentenschutz, Vienna*.

Bonsang, E. (2009). Does informal care from children to their elderly parents substitute for formal care in Europe? *Journal of Health Economics*, *28*(1), 143–154. https://doi.org/10.1016/j.jhealeco.2008.09.002

Borderies, F., Amar, E., & Leroux, I. (2016). Les bénéficiaires de l'aide sociale départementale en 2014. *Direction de la recherche, des études, de l'évaluation et des statistiques. Série Statistiques, n° 200*.

Börsch-Supan, A. (2017). *Survey of Health, Ageing and Retirement in Europe (SHARE) Wave 6. Release version: 6.0.0*.

Börsch-Supan, A., Brandt, M., Hunkler, C., Kneip, T., Korbmacher, J., Malter, F., … Zuber, S. (2013). Data Resource Profile: The Survey of Health, Ageing and Retirement in Europe (SHARE). *International Journal of Epidemiology*, *42*(4), 992–1001. https://doi.org/10.1093/ije/dyt088

Bound, J. (1991). Self-reported versus objective measures of health in retirement models. *Journal of Human Resources*, *26*, 106–138. https://doi.org/10.2307/145718

Bundesamt, S. (2015). *Pflegestatistik 2013. Pflege im Rahmen der Pflegeversicherung Deutschlandergebnisse*. Wiesbaden: Statistisches Bundesamt.

Carrino, L., & Orso, C. E. (2015). Eligibility regulations and formal home-care utilisation among the vulnerable older people in SHARE Wave 5. In A. Börsch-Supan, T. Kneip, H. Litwin, M. Myck, & G. Weber (Eds.), *Ageing in Europe-supporting policies for an inclusive society* (Vol. 343). Berlin: Walter de Gruyter Gmbh & Co.

Castro-Costa, E., Dewey, M., Stewart, R., Banerjee, S., Huppert, F., Mendonca-Lima, C., … Prince, M. (2007). Prevalence of depressive symptoms and syndromes in later life in ten European countries: The SHARE study. *The British Journal of Psychiatry*, *191*, 393–401. https://doi.org/10.1192/bjp.bp.107.036772

Chan, K. S., Kasper, J. D., Brandt, J., & Pezzin, L. E. (2012). Measurement equivalence in ADL and IADL difficulty across international surveys of aging: Findings From the HRS, SHARE, and ELSA. *The Journals of Gerontology Series B: Psychological Sciences and Social Sciences*, *67B*(1), 121–132. https://doi.org/10.1093/geronb/gbr133

Colombo, F., Llena-Nozal, A., Mercier, J., & Tjadens, F. (2011). *OECD Health Policy Studies Help Wanted? Providing and Paying for Long-Term Care: Providing and Paying for Long-Term Care* (Vol. 2011): OECD Publishing.

Colombo, F., & Mercier, J. (2012). Help wanted? Fair and sustainable financing of long-term care services. *Applied Economic Perspectives and Policy, 34*(2), 316–332.

Comas-Herrera, A., Costa-i-Font, J., Gori, C., di Maio, A., Patxot, C., Pickard, L., …, Wittenberg, R. (2003). *European study of long-term care expenditure: Investigating the sensitivity of projections of future long-term care expenditure in Germany, Spain, Italy and the United Kingdom to changes in assumptions about demography, dependency, informal care, formal care and unit costs* (Report to the European Commission, Employment and Social Affairs DG, PSSRU Discussion Paper 1840).

Comas-Herrera, A., Wittenberg, R., Costa-Font, J., Gori, C., Di Maio, A., Patxot, C., … Rothgang, H. (2006). Future long-term care expenditure in Germany, Spain, Italy and the United Kingdom. *Ageing and Society, 26*(02), 285–302.

Costa-Font, J., Courbage, C., & Swartz, K. (2015). Financing long-term care: Ex ante, ex post or both? *Health Economics, 24*, 45–57. https://doi.org/10.1002/hec.3152

Costa-Font, J., Wittenberg, R., Patxot, C., Comas-Herrera, A., Gori, C., di Maio, A., … Rothgang, H. (2008). Projecting long-term care expenditure in four European Union member states: The influence of demographic scenarios. *Social Indicators Research, 86*(2), 303–321.

de Meijer, C., Bakx, P., van Doorslaer, E., & Koopmanschap, M. (2015). Explaining declining rates of institutional LTC Use in The Netherlands: A decomposition approach. *Health Economics, 24*, 18–31. https://doi.org/10.1002/hec.3114

de Meijer, C., Koopmanschap, M., d'Uva, T. B., & van Doorslaer, E. (2011). Determinants of long-term care spending: Age, time to death or disability? *Journal of Health Economics, 30*(2), 425–438. https://doi.org/10.1016/j.jhealeco.2010.12.010

de Meijer, C., Majer, I., Koopmanschap, M., & van Baal, P. (2012). Forecasting lifetime and aggregate long-term care spending: Accounting for changing disability patterns. *Medical Care, 50*(8), 722–729.

Dewey, M. E., & Prince, M. J. (2005). Mental health. In A. Börsch-Supan & H. Jürges (Eds.), *Health, ageing and retirement in Europe—First results from the Survey of Health, Ageing and Retirement in Europe* (Vol. SHARE Codebook 8). Mannheim: MEA Eigenverlag.

Dwyer, D. S., & Mitchell, O. S. (1999). Health problems as determinants of retirement: Are self-rated measures endogenous? *Journal of Health Economics, 18*(2), 173–193. https://doi.org/10.3386/w6503

EUROSTAT. (2015). The 2012 Ageing report: Economic and budgetary projections for the 28 EU Member States (2013–2060).

Gerkens, S., & Merkur, S. (2010). Belgium: Health system review. *Health Systems in Transition*, *12*(5), 1–266.

Gori, C., & Fernandez, J.-L. (2015). *Long-term care reforms in OECD countries.* Bristol: Policy Press.

Gravelle, H. (2003). Measuring income related inequality in health: Standardisation and the partial concentration index. *Health Economics*, *12*(10), 803–819.

Jiménez-Martín, S., & Prieto, C. V. (2012). The trade-off between formal and informal care in Spain. *The European Journal of Health Economics*, *13*(4), 461–490.

Kalwij, A., Pasini, G., & Wu, M. (2014). Home care for the elderly: The role of relatives, friends and neighbors. *Review of Economics of the Household*, *12*(2), 379–404. https://doi.org/10.1007/s11150-012-9159-4

Kapteyn, A., & Meijer, E. (2013). A Comparison of different measures of health and their relation to labor force transitions at older ages. In *Discoveries in the Economics of Aging* (pp. 115–150). University of Chicago Press.

Karakaya, G. (2009). Long-term care: regional disparities in Belgium. *Journal of Applied Economic Sciences*, *4*(7).

Katz, S., Downs, T. D., Cash, H. R., & Grotz, R. C. (1970). Progress in development of the index of ADL. *The Gerontologist*, *10*(1 Part 1), 20–30. https://doi.org/10.1093/geront/10.1_Part_1.20

Kim, H. B., & Lim, W. (2015). Long-term care insurance, informal care, and medical expenditures. *Journal of Public Economics*, *125*, 128–142. https://doi.org/10.1016/j.jpubeco.2014.12.004

LaFortune, G., & Balestat, G. (2007). *Trends in severe disability among elderly people. Assessing the evidence in 12 OECD countries and the future implications.* OECD Health Working Papers. https://doi.org/10.1787/217072070078.

LaPlante, M. P. (2010). The classic measure of disability in activities of daily living is biased by age but an expanded IADL/ADL measure is not. *The Journals of Gerontology Series B: Psychological Sciences and Social Sciences*, *65*(6), 720–732. https://doi.org/10.1093/geronb/gbp129

Lawton, M. P., & Brody, E. M. (1969). Assessment of older people: Self-maintaining and instrumental activities of daily living. *The Gerontologist*, *9*(3).

Maggino, F., & Zumbo, B. (2012). Measuring the quality of life and the construction of social indicators. In K. C. Land, A. C. Michalos, & M. J. Sirgy (Eds.), *Handbook of social indicators and quality of life research* (pp. 201–238). Netherlands: Springer.

Manton, K. G., Lamb, V. L., & Gu, X. L. (2007). Medicare cost effects of recent US disability trends in the elderly: Future implications. *Journal of Aging and Health*, *19*(3).

Marmot, M., Oldfield, Z., Clemens, S., Blake, M., Phelps, A., Nazroo, J., …, Oskala, A. (2016). English longitudinal study of ageing: Waves 0–7, 1998–2015. 26th Edition. *UK Data Service. SN: 5050*. https://doi.org/10.5255/UKDA-SN-5050-13

OECD. (2011). *Long-term care country profile: Austria*. Paris: OECD publishing. https://www.oecd.org/austria/47877397.pdf

OECD. (2016). *Health at a glance: OECD indicators*. Paris: OECD Publishing.

Peña-Longobardo, L. M., Oliva-Moreno, J., García-Armesto, S., & Hernández-Quevedo, C. (2016). The Spanish long-term care system in transition: Ten years since the 2006 Dependency Act. *Health Policy, 120*(10), 1177–1182. https://doi.org/10.1016/j.healthpol.2016.08.012

Pickard, L., Comas-Herrera, A., Costa-Font, J., Gori, C., di Maio, A., Patxot, C., … Wittenberg, R. (2007). Modelling an entitlement to long-term care services for older people in Europe: Projections for long-term care expenditure to 2050. *Journal of European Social Policy, 17*(1), 33–48.

Riedel, M., & Kraus, M. (2010). The Austrian long-term care system. *ENEPRI Research Report, 69*.

Schokkaert, E., & Van de Voorde, C. (2009). Direct versus indirect standardization in risk adjustment. *Journal of Health Economics, 28*(2), 361–374.

Schultz, E. (2010). *The long-term care system for the elderly in Germany: ENEPRI Research Report*.

Verbeek-Oudijk, D., Woittiez, I., Eggink, E., & Putman, L. (2014). *Who cares in Europe? A comparison of long-term care for the over 50s in sixteen European countries*. Den Haag (NL): Institute for Social Research.

White, J., Zaninotto, P., Walters, K., Kivimäki, M., Demakakos, P., Biddulph, J., … Batty, G. D. (2016). Duration of depressive symptoms and mortality risk: The English Longitudinal Study of Ageing (ELSA). *The British Journal of Psychiatry, 208*(4), 337–342. https://doi.org/10.1192/bjp.bp.114.155333

Willemé, P. (2010). The long-term care system for the elderly in Belgium. *ENEPRI Research Report* (70).

CHAPTER 5

Life-Course Health and Inequality

Abstract In Chap. 5, we address the "health equity" issue related to the access to formal home care services across a set of European countries. We make use of the individual-level eligibility index developed in Chap. 4, and relate it to the most relevant "covariates". The novelty of this chapter is that, by using the SHARE and the ELSA data, we can analyse the effect of adverse health shocks occurring during individuals' lives as captured by a cumulative measure of health deterioration. The purpose of the analysis is to compare individuals with similar socio-economic backgrounds and similar health histories, by distinguishing those who may face the need for LTC as a result of a health shock: this is the "demand side" of the programme. However, depending on the LTC regulation to which these individuals are exposed, they will have different probabilities of access to care and different coverage, i.e., there is also a "supply side". We describe how different LTC systems cope with the "cumulative health disadvantage".

Keywords Demand for care • Health shocks • Chronic diseases • Health equity • Cumulative health disadvantage

In the previous chapters (namely Chaps. 2 and 3), we described in detail the different LTC systems operating in Europe by emphasizing how the different rules may shape welfare and care provisions for older individuals. We looked at both the eligibility conditions for LTC, i.e., whether a programme includes specific limitations in the vulnerability assessment hence

A. Brugiavini et al., *Vulnerability and Long-term Care in Europe*,
https://doi.org/10.1007/978-3-319-68969-2_5

determining the "extensive margin" and the system of weights attached to each limitation in defining a need-of-care scale (explaining the generosity of the programme or the "intensive margin").

In this chapter, we address more directly the "health equity" issue related to the access to formal home care services across a set of European countries, which have been documented as highly heterogeneous in terms of LTC legislations. We make use of the eligibility index measured at the individual level for access to LTC programmes as developed in Chap. 4. The index allows us to estimate the share of population aged 65+ that would be eligible for home care services implemented in the country/region of residence at the time of the interview and relate this outcome to the most relevant "covariates". The novelty of the present chapter is that, by using the SHARE and the ELSA data, we can analyse the effect of adverse health shocks occurring during individuals' lives as captured by cumulative measures of health deterioration. We can account for the onset of specific health conditions such as cancer, cardiovascular diseases, diabetes, arthritis and osteoporosis over the life-course: this is a unique feature of the longitudinal data we exploit in our research. The aim of the analysis is to compare individuals with similar socio-economic backgrounds and similar health histories, by distinguishing those who may face the need for LTC as a result of a health shock: this is the "demand side" of the programme. However, depending on the LTC legislations these individuals to which these are exposed, they will have different probabilities of access to care and different coverage, i.e., there is also a "supply side". We describe how different LTC systems cope with the "cumulative health disadvantage".

5.1 Cumulative Health Measures in SHARE and ELSA

Improved living conditions, better prevention, and technological advances in medical interventions have supported the increased longevity of the population in most western countries. Scientists are debating whether, parallel to this trend, there exists a "compression of morbidity" or, at the extreme, an "expansion of morbidity", i.e., an increase in the number of years in poor health conditions and/or a higher prevalence of diseases. Indeed, over the last decades, we have witnessed a slow, but persistent increase in chronic diseases and chronic conditions for older people in Europe, requiring long spells of medical treatment and care. Thanks to the availability of information in the SHARE survey and the ELSA survey we are in a unique position to investigate how different European LTC systems cope with the "cumulative health disadvantage". To be more precise, in this chapter, we analyse the effect of adverse health shocks occurring during individual's lives on the probability of being eligible to LTC programmes by adopting standard econometric techniques.

5.1.1 Data and Variables

The SHARE and ELSA surveys[1] have been designed by following the format of their "sister" study in the USA, the Health and Retirement Study (HRS). They are almost identical to the HRS with respect to survey design, longitudinal dimension, interview target population, and topics coverage (Börsch-Supan & Jürges, 2005; Taylor et al., 2007). The SHARE study collects detailed longitudinal information on a wide variety of aspects, among which health status, access to health care and socio-economic characteristics of people aged 50 or older (and their spouses/partners) in 27 European countries, plus Israel (Börsch-Supan & Jürges, 2005). It started in 2004 and it is carried out bi-annually.[2] The ELSA study collects panel data from a representative sample of the English population aged 50+, and younger spouses/partners: the sample is drawn from respondents to the Health Survey for England and covers around 12,000 men and women, interviewed every other year.

In our analysis, we use the two more recent waves of SHARE (wave 6, 2015) and ELSA (wave 7, 2014/2015), respectively. Several health-related measures in SHARE parallel those in ELSA or can be adapted in order to allow for cross-country comparisons (Taylor et al., 2003). As mentioned in Chap. 4 (Sect. 4.1), the two surveys contain comparable information on chronic conditions and symptoms reported by the respondents, and the age at which these conditions have been diagnosed by a doctor for the first time. This feature of the data allows us to pinpoint the time of onset of the chronic condition and to perform a life-course analysis in terms of the risk of exposure to a given condition. We focus on a set of commonly used measures of chronic conditions, which have been documented in the medical literature to be of particular relevance (Banks, Marmot, Oldfield, & Smith, 2006; Yach, Hawkes, Gould, & Hofman, 2004), such as cancer, cardiovascular conditions (heart attack and stroke), diabetes and arthritis, plus the age at which the disease has been diagnosed for the first time. By counting the number of years in which each condition was present, we generate a set of individual continuous variables measuring the years of exposure to each specific disease.

In addition to these cumulative health measures, we also control for the presence of multiple chronic conditions (multi-morbidity) which is well known to be a specific feature of frailty and vulnerability in old age (Fabbri et al., 2015). To be more precise, multi-morbidity is defined as the number of chronic diseases an individual suffers from at the time of the interview, and the measure is a simple count of such health conditions. This indicator concerns a set of self-reported chronic diseases such as heart problems, high blood pressure, stroke, diabetes, lung disease, arthritis/osteoporosis and cancer. Crucially for our analysis, we employ the individual-specific eligibility index—computed for individuals participating in the last waves of SHARE and ELSA—as a proxy for the potential access for formal home care services. This index, as described in detail in Chap. 4, identifies individuals who are eligible for public formal home care based on LTC legislations implemented in their area of residence. Our analysis focuses on a sample of countries were LTC rules are *carer-blind,* and no role is played by other factors like the availability of informal care, the family environment, the wider social network or the neighbourhood (Eleftheriades & Wittenberg, 2013). The countries included are: Austria, Belgium (divided into Flanders Wallonia and Brussels), Germany, France, the Czech Republic, England and Wales, and Spain.

To complete the analysis and to control for other relevant characteristics we include demographic variables and socio-economic indicators, for example we use as explanatory variables the age of respondents and their level of education. The level of education is particularly relevant in this literature as it may serve as a proxy—to some extent—for individual skills (Mazzonna, 2014; Sirin, 2005) as well as general knowledge and ability to process information: these characteristics facilitate access to resources and to care as well as healthy behaviour. The level of education in SHARE and ELSA is measured by the ISCED-1997 classification. Three levels of education are considered: (1) low education (no educational certificates or primary school certificate or lower secondary education); (2) medium education (upper secondary education or high school graduation); (3) high education (university degree or postgraduate).

Our final sample includes 21,301 individuals aged 65 and older, as they represent the potential target of the LTC interventions. The characteristics of the sample are summarized in Table 5.1 (separately by gender).

The left-hand side of Table 5.1 reports summary statistics on the prevalence of the set of chronic conditions considered in the analysis: health

Table 5.1 Descriptive statistics

	Prevalence of chronic diseases				*Years of exposure to chronic diseases, conditioned to having any*			
	Male		*Female*		*Male*		*Female*	
	Mean	*S.D.*	*Mean*	*S.D.*	*Mean*	*S.D.*	*Mean*	*S.D.*
	N = 9644		*N = 11,657*		*N = 4194*		*N = 4992*	
Eligibility	0.09	0.29	0.13	0.33	0.15	0.36	0.20	0.40
Age	73.72	6.35	74.23	6.61	74.83	6.38	75.54	6.66
Education:								
Low	0.35	0.47	0.47	0.49	0.36	0.48	0.52	0.49
Medium	0.40	0.49	0.37	0.48	0.42	0.49	0.36	0.48
High	0.24	0.42	0.14	0.35	0.21	0.41	0.11	0.31
Chronic conditions:								
Cancer	0.07	0.25	0.05	0.22	17.07	11.52	16.49	10.56
Stroke	0.06	0.23	0.04	0.20	15.64	10.54	18.17	12.45
Heart attack	0.15	0.36	0.10	0.30	19.00	12.57	21.64	14.96
Arthritis	0.23	0.42	0.37	0.48	22.39	13.37	22.86	14.34
Diabetes	0.19	0.39	0.15	0.36	18.83	11.67	19.15	11.46
Number of chronic diseases	1.26	1.08	1.28	1.06	2.03	0.99	1.98	1.01

Source: SHARE wave 6, Releases 6.0.0. ELSA, wave 7. Number of obs.: 21301. Countries: Austria, Germany, France, Belgium Flanders, Belgium Wallonia, the Czech Republic, England and Wales

conditions are measured by dummy variables indicating the presence of a specific disease at the time of the interview. The right-hand side of Table 5.1 refers to the subsample of respondents reporting at least one year of exposure to a specific chronic health condition during their lives. In this case, the length of the chronic disease is measured by a continuous variable indicating the years of exposure to a specific disorder.

Regarding the prevalence of chronic health conditions, heart attack, arthritis and diabetes are the most common disorders, with a prevalence of 57 per cent for males and 62 per cent for females, respectively. All other conditions (cancer and stroke) are less frequent (9 per cent for females, 13 per cent for males). The prevalence of cardiovascular diseases, cancer and diabetes does not display important gender differences, while the frequency of rheumatologic disorders like arthritis is higher in women than in men (around 37 per cent against 23 per cent). The mean number of chronic diseases in both subsamples is around 1.2, ranging from 1 to 7. If we look at the subsamples of individuals reporting at least one year of exposure to chronic diseases (the right-hand side of Table 5.1), we note that, in general, both male and female respondents share similar characteristics in terms of years of exposure to cancer, diabetes and arthritis. Regarding cardiovascular diseases, the average years of exposure for males is around 34, slightly lower than the figure for female respondents (approximately 39). As for the average number of chronic conditions, we do not observe significant differences by gender: the mean number of chronic diseases is around two for both groups.

Tables 5.2 and 5.3 present some additional statistics with a special focus on cumulative health conditions according to the eligibility status of respondents.

A first inspection of Tables 5.2 and 5.3 reveals that the fraction of respondents with a lower prevalence of chronic conditions is observed in the "non-eligible group" compared to the "eligible group". For instance,

Table 5.2 Summary statistics, eligible subsample

	Prevalence of chronic diseases				*Years of exposure to chronic diseases, conditioned to having any*			
	Male		*Female*		*Male*		*Female*	
	Mean	*S.D.*	*Mean*	*S.D.*	*Mean*	*S.D.*	*Mean*	*S.D.*
	N = 923		*N = 1521*		*N = 643*		*N = 1004*	
Age	77.35	6.86	79.00	6.88	77.23	6.70	78.95	6.76
Education:								
Low	0.49	0.50	0.63	0.48	0.46	0.49	0.62	0.48
Medium	0.36	0.48	0.29	0.45	0.39	0.48	0.31	0.46
High	0.14	0.34	0.06	0.25	0.14	0.35	0.05	0.23
Chronic conditions:								
Cancer	0.11	0.32	0.06	0.25	20.23	14.09	18.36	9.93
Stroke	0.17	0.37	0.12	0.33	15.52	9.88	19.87	13.82
Heart attack	0.25	0.43	0.19	0.39	20.10	14.30	22.49	14.91
Arthritis	0.38	0.48	0.54	0.49	23.16	13.66	24.68	15.10
Diabetes	0.28	0.45	0.25	0.43	19.95	11.30	22.53	12.58
Number of chronic diseases	1.96	1.25	1.87	1.19	2.44	1.09	2.34	1.07

Source: SHARE wave 6, Releases 6.0.0. ELSA, wave 7. Number of obs.: 2444. Countries: Austria, Germany, France, Belgium Flanders, Belgium Wallonia, the Czech Republic, England and Wales

Table 5.3 Summary statistics, non-eligible subsample

	Prevalence of chronic diseases				*Years of exposure to chronic diseases, conditioned to having any*			
	Male		*Female*		*Male*		*Female*	
	Mean	*S.D.*	*Mean*	*S.D.*	*Mean*	*S.D.*	*Mean*	*S.D.*
	N = 8721		*N = 10,136*		*N = 3551*		*N = 3988*	
Age	73.33	6.17	73.51	6.26	74.39	6.22	74.69	6.36
Education:								
Low	0.34	0.47	0.45	.049	0.34	0.47	0.49	0.50
Medium	0.40	0.49	0.38	0.48	0.42	0.49	0.38	0.48
High	0.25	0.43	0.15	0.36	0.22	0.41	0.12	0.32
Chronic conditions:								
Cancer	0.06	0.24	0.05	0.21	16.42	10.82	16.12	10.66
Stroke	0.048	0.21	0.03	0.17	15.69	10.81	17.10	11.40
Heart attack	0.14	0.35	0.08	0.28	18.79	12.21	21.37	14.97
Arthritis	0.21	0.41	0.35	0.47	22.18	13.30	22.32	14.07
Diabetes	0.18	0.38	0.14	0.35	18.30	11.72	18.27	10.98
Number of chronic diseases	1.18	1.04	1.19	1.01	1.96	0.96	1.89	0.98

Source: SHARE wave 6, Releases 6.0.0. ELSA, wave 7. Number of obs.: 18,857. Countries: Austria, Germany, France, Belgium Flanders, Belgium Wallonia, the Czech Republic, England and Wales

roughly 18 per cent of male non-eligible respondents declare themselves as suffering from diabetes, compared with 28 per cent of male respondents in the eligible subsample. Similarly, 21 per cent of the non-eligible males have arthritis, compared to 38 per cent of eligible individuals. The same applies for the subsample of individuals reporting at least one year of exposure to chronic conditions: the average number of years of exposure to chronic diseases is higher for the eligible respondents compared to the non-eligible ones.

5.2 Inequality in Long-Term Care Services Access: A Multivariate Analysis

The descriptive evidence discussed in Sect. 5.1 is based on a simple disaggregation of the samples into homogenous groups, some of these exogenously determined, for example the two subsamples split by gender.

However, the evidence on the "eligible" group versus the "non- eligible" group of Table 5.3 is addressing precisely the issue under investigation, but several confounding factors may be affecting the results. Since we are interested in uncovering how different LTC legislations cope with the cumulative health disadvantage, we need to assess the association between the eligibility status of respondents, as a proxy for the potential access to formal home care programmes, and the years of exposure to specific chronic diseases. We think that from a methodological point of view it is appropriate to carry out a multivariate analysis, which allows us to focus on the relevant variables controlling for the other characteristics of the respondents to the surveys.

To assess the association between the eligibility status of respondents (as a proxy for the potential access to home care programmes) and the years of exposure to specific chronic diseases along the life-course, we consider a set of econometric specifications which fall under the broad classification of "linear probability model", where we relate, in a linear way, the eligibility variable to its determinants. The dependent variable is the dichotomous "eligibility index" described in detail in Chap. 4, which takes value 1 if eligibility is recorded or value 0 otherwise. We additionally control for demographics and socio-economic characteristics of respondents (age, education) besides gender; however, we are concerned that some of the institutional effects of the country of residence (say, other provisions) may play a role. In order to account for unobserved country-specific effects, we include country dummies in all regressions. Results are provided in Tables 5.4, 5.5, 5.6.

Our results suggest that the Age variable and the Education variable have the expected effect: as individuals age, the probability of being eligible increases, and the growth rate itself also increases. This means that the oldest of the old are extremely likely to be in need of LTC services. Education has the well-known "protective role": low-educated men have a 4 per cent higher probability of being eligible for LTC services than medium- and higher-educated males. The effect is similar for women. As regards the country dummies, controlling for age, education and exposure to chronic diseases there are no statistically significant differences (at the 5 % level) between the Austrian, Spanish, German, French and Czech respondents. On the other hand, being an English or Welsh citizen increases the probability of being eligible by 2.7 per cent for males and by 5.5 per cent for females, while living in Belgium reduces the probability of being eligible.

Table 5.4 Linear probability estimates of the eligibility status

Dependent Variable:		
Eligible (yes/no)	*Sample of males 65+*	
	Coeff.	*S.E.*
Age	−0.0718***	0.0126
Age2	0.0005***	0.0001
Low_education	0.0409***	0.0082
High_education	−0.0101	0.0065
Exposure to:		
Cancer (years)	0.0015*	0.0008
Stroke (years)	0.0041***	0.0011
Hearth attack (years)	−0.0002	0.0004
Arthritis (years)	0.0023***	0.0004
Diabetes (years)	−0.0001	0.0004
# Chronic diseases	0.040***	0.0041
Country-dummies:		
Germany	−0.0069	0.0113
Spain	−0.0219*	0.0122
France	0.0091	0.0131
Czech Republic	−0.0042	0.0119
England and Wales	0.0271**	0.0108
Belgium_Flanders	−0.0544***	0.0113
Belgium_Wallonia	−0.0481***	0.0124

Source: SHARE wave 6, Releases 6.0.0. ELSA, wave 7. Countries: Austria, Germany, Spain, France, the Czech Republic, England and Wales, Belgium Flanders, Belgium Wallonia. *** p-value<0.01, ** p-value <0.05, * p-value <0.1

The key results are represented by the coefficients of "Years of exposure to chronic diseases" on the probability of being eligible for LTC services. Having being previously diagnosed with a stroke or arthritis increases the likelihood of being vulnerable after age 65 both for men and women. Moreover, males that report a cancer diagnosis in the past and females with diabetes are more likely to be eligible. Finally, multi-morbidity as reported in the literature is an important driver of vulnerability: every additional chronic disease increases the probability of being eligible by 4 per cent for men and by 3.4 per cent for women.

Table 5.6 allows to better appreciate the magnitude of the effects of the parameters of interest: we report the marginal effects on the probability of being eligible after 65 of an additional year of exposure to a chronic disease—compared to mean years of exposure. One extra year of exposure,

Table 5.5 Linear probability estimates of eligibility status

Dependent variable:		
Eligible (yes/no)	*Sample of females 65+*	
	Coeff.	*S.E.*
Age	−0.1305***	0.0119
Age2	0.0009***	0.0001
Low_education	0.0370***	0.0072
High_education	−0.0101	0.0073
Exposure to:		
Cancer (years)	−0.0001	0.0008
Stroke (years)	0.0060***	0.0010
Hearth attack (years)	0.0001	0.0005
Arthritis (years)	0.0017	0.0003
Diabetes (years)	0.0016***	0.0005
# Chronic diseases	0.0345***	0.0039
Country-dummies:		
Germany	−0.0014	0.0108
Spain	0.0190	0.0118
France	0.0149	0.0118
Czech Republic	0.0181*	0.0105
England and Wales	0.0558***	0.0103
Belgium_Flanders	−0.0369***	0.0113
Belgium_Wallonia	−0.0236*	0.0129

Source: SHARE wave 6, Releases 6.0.0. ELSA, wave 7. Countries: Austria, Germany, Spain, France, the Czech Republic, England and Wales, Belgium Flanders, Belgium Wallonia. ***p-value <0.01, **p-value <0.05, *p-value <0.1

compared to the mean years of exposure for the respondents who had a stroke, increases the chances of being eligible by 6.43 per cent for males and by almost 11 per cent for females. The marginal effects associated to other chronic diseases (in Table 5.6 we report only the statistically significant effects) are smaller, but still relevant.

Our results show a strong association between cumulative exposure to chronic conditions and eligibility to LTC, which confirms the important insurance role of LTC. It is also interesting to note that the onset of a chronic disease represents an "early warning" with respect to the probability of being vulnerable at older ages: years of exposure to one or several chronic diseases increase substantially the probability of being eligible at older ages. In this respect, our measures signal the relevance of prevention in the general approach to health care for older people.

Table 5.6 Marginal effects of an additional year of exposure to a chronic disease on a probability to be eligible

	Male (%)	*Female (%)*
Exposure to:		
Cancer	2.56	
Stroke	6.43	10.90
Heart Attack		
Arthritis	5.15	3.89
Diabetes		3.06

Source: SHARE wave 6, Releases 6.0.0. ELSA, wave 7. Countries: Austria, Germany, Spain, France, the Czech Republic, England and Wales, Belgium Flanders, Belgium Wallonia

Notes

1. For a detailed description of the surveys, see Chap. 4.
2. SHARE is coordinated by the Munich Research Institute for the Economics of Aging (MEA).

References

Banks, J., Marmot, M., Oldfield, Z., & Smith, J. P. (2006). Disease and disadvantage in the United States and in England. *JAMA*, *295*(17), 2037–2045.

Börsch-Supan, A., & Jürges, H. (2005). *The Survey of Health, Ageing and Retirement in Europe—Methodology*. Mannheim: MEA.

Eleftheriades, C., & Wittenberg, R. (2013). *A critical review of international practice on assessment and eligibility in adult social care: Lessons for England*. Oxford: Centre for Health Service Economics & Organisation (CHSEO).

Fabbri, E., Zoli, M., Gonzalez-Freire, M., Salive, M. E., Studenski, S. A., & Ferrucci, L. (2015). Aging and multimorbidity: New tasks, priorities, and frontiers for integrated gerontological and clinical research. *Journal of the American Medical Directors Association*, *16*(8), 640–647.

Mazzonna, F. (2014). The long lasting effects of education on old age health: Evidence of gender differences. *Social Science & Medicine*, *101*, 129–138.

Sirin, S. R. (2005). Socioeconomic status and academic achievement: A meta-analytic review of research. *Review of Educational Research*, *75*(3), 417–453.

Taylor, R., Conway, L., Calderwood, L., Lessof, C., Cheshire, H., Cox, K., & Scholes, S. (2007). *Health, wealth and lifestyles of the older population in England: The 2002 English Longitudinal Study of Ageing; Technical Report*. London: Institute of Fiscal Studies.

Taylor, R., Conway, L., Caldenwood, L., Lessof, C., Marmot, J., Banks, R., … Nazroo, J. (2003). *Methodology. Health, wealth, and lifestyles of the older population in England: The 2002 English Longitudinal Study of Ageing* (pp. 357–374). London: The Institute for Fiscal Studies.

Yach, D., Hawkes, C., Gould, C. L., & Hofman, K. J. (2004). The global burden of chronic diseases: Overcoming impediments to prevention and control. *JAMA*, *291*(21), 2616–2622.

CHAPTER 6

Conclusions

Abstract This chapter offers some concluding remarks on the analyses and results obtained in this book. We have critically reviewed the long-term care (LTC) systems operating in Europe by offering a detailed taxonomy of the concept of vulnerability and its applied counterpart. We have described the evaluation protocols adopted in the various countries when granting access to care to older claimants. The multidimensional nature of the concept of vulnerability, in the absence of a unique and standardized definition, generates substantial differences in the assessment-of-need and eligibility conditions across Europe. This heterogeneity in LTC programmes implies that coverage, benefit generosity and allowances may be very different even for neighbouring countries to the extent that different groups of older people may experience difference levels of well-being as a result.

Keywords Ageing • Long-term care eligibility criteria • Vulnerability • Long-term care coverage • Health equity

This book has reviewed the long-term care (LTC) systems operating in Europe by offering a detailed taxonomy of the concept of vulnerability and how this is operationalized through the evaluation protocols, which are adopted in different countries to grant access to care to older claimants. The multidimensional nature of the concept of vulnerability, in the absence of a unique and standardized definition, generates substantial

A. Brugiavini et al., *Vulnerability and Long-term Care in Europe*,
https://doi.org/10.1007/978-3-319-68969-2_6

differences in the assessment-of-need and eligibility conditions across Europe. This heterogeneity in LTC programmes implies that coverage, benefit generosity and allowances may differ substantially from country to country or even for different groups of the population within the same country, thus creating a *patchwork* of welfare interventions.

We first introduced the concept of vulnerability and explained how this has evolved in the different socio-economic frameworks; we then turned the attention to the medical literature which has provided benchmarks and elaborated tools to measure different degrees of vulnerability. In particular, we discussed the role played by measures such as "limitations in activities of daily living" (ADL), which point to the "functioning" of the individual rather than to the "lack of illnesses", when discriminating between vulnerable and non-vulnerable individuals.

Chapters 2 and 3 provided a very detailed taxonomy of the measurement of vulnerability adopted in the various European countries or regions: the most striking feature is the wide variability prevailing even at the regional level, such as in the case of Italy. We offered a description of the dimensions/items used in the different programmes to assess eligibility for LTC, which range from limitation in ADL, to cognitive impairment or even general welfare conditions within the household. A very peculiar characteristic of some LTC systems is that they are *care-sighted* rather than *care-blind*, i.e., they take into account the actions of the caregiver in order to grant access to benefits. A further source of variability is the way in which each LTC system attaches weights to each dimension/item in order to produce a summary measure: an index or a score of vulnerability. In all these systems, individuals are deemed eligible for the benefit if their score is above a given threshold: some countries fix rather low thresholds so that their LTC system is more inclusive, while other countries are more concerned with individuals who are severely disabled and in need of substantial care, hence placing the threshold at higher levels of the index.

The novelty of our research is that we can make use of micro-data at the individual level recorded in two large surveys: the English Longitudinal Study on Ageing (ELSA) survey in England and the Survey of Health Ageing and Retirement in Europe (SHARE) study in the rest of Europe. In order to provide a first indication of how the data can be exploited to gain information on the impact of LTC provisions, in Chap. 3 we provide detailed descriptions of the rules in place in each country along with the corresponding item/variable recorded in the datasets. For example, both

ELSA and SHARE record limitations in ADL which match very closely most items used in the assessment-of-need protocols.

Chapter 4 expanded even further the use of the micro-data from ELSA and SHARE by estimating the potential coverage of each specific LTC programme on the sample individuals who are interviewed (respondents) in each country. A first description of the LTC systems is provided by presenting "crude rates", i.e., the share of the sample which we predict as eligible for care on the basis of the legislation prevailing in each country. In order to examine, in detail, the relationship between eligibility rules and access to care, we propose a methodology which allows to disentangle the effect of the sample composition (population effect) from the effects of the actual legislation on coverage rates. More precisely, by applying the battery of rules envisaged by each system on a "standard European population" from the SHARE and ELSA studies, we generate a set of comparable eligibility rates. These are called "directly-adjusted" rates because they are computed as the share of the eligible individuals over the standard population at risk. Furthermore, we perform pair-wise comparisons of coverage rates through a counterfactual analysis, also known as "indirect adjustment". In this latter case we simulated the application of the rules of one country to the population of the other countries and showed that eligibility rules which directly account for iADL (alongside ADL) imply higher coverage rates. Similarly, higher inclusiveness is generated by assessment strategies which evaluate the vulnerability status through the accumulation of functional deficits or through the presence of cognitive limitations. We pointed out how each definition of vulnerability identifies a very specific "eligible target population": even when two programmes end up with identical coverage rates, the individuals who are regarded as eligible in each programme may exhibit very different characteristics. This discrepancy is driven by the inclusion/exclusion of specific outcomes in the assessment-of-need and by the different weighting of the single outcomes in determining the eligibility status.

A further development is presented in Chap. 5, where we analysed the effect of adverse health shocks occurring during individuals' lives as captured by a cumulative measures of health deterioration. Thanks to the richness and unique features of the ELSA and SHARE longitudinal data, we can account for the onset of specific health conditions such as cancer, cardiovascular diseases, diabetes, arthritis and osteoporosis over the life-course of individuals. This application allowed us to compare individuals with similar socio-economic backgrounds and similar health histories, who may face different LTC systems at different points of their life. The methodology delivers a "robust" statistical estimate of the potential demand for the different LTC programmes, as it takes account of the health history of individuals and actual exposure to different welfare interventions. Depending on the LTC rules in place, these individuals have different probabilities of gaining access to care and can benefit from different levels of coverage. We discuss how LTC systems cope with the "cumulative health disadvantage" that these shocks generate over the life-course, considering also the role played by preventive care and preventive actions.

The book has shown that there is scope for harmonization both on terms of assessment-of-needs procedures and in terms of long-term care provisions. The assessment procedures of each country or region are largely affected by sluggish and often-complex legislation, with little attention to the fast-changing health conditions of older people, to the extent that many countries ignore cognitive impairments in their protocols while cognitive decline is becoming a major source of dependency. Long-term care insurance is extremely fragmented and a significant variability of benefits and provisions emerges even at a local level. We argued that there is a lot to learn from the experience of the other countries and also from empirical work carried out at the micro level in Europe and in each country. We show that by taking into account not only the health domain, but also the socio-economic characteristics of the older person as well as the characteristics of her/his household, we can identify the most effective methodologies to provide a robust assessment-of-needs as well as the efficacy of the different policies in providing good care and ultimately guaranteeing well-being to older people.

Appendix

ADL and iADL[1]

The ADL taxonomy assesses how an individual performs, without assistance, in six main functioning domains: bathing, dressing, toileting, transferring, continence and feeding. The iADL scale comprises eight tasks: ability to use the telephone, shopping, food preparation, housekeeping, doing laundry, mode of transportation, responsibility for own medications and ability to handle finances. In being performed, the activities included in the iADL list require a more complex of neuropsychological organization than ADL, and therefore measure less severe levels of vulnerability.[2] Brief definitions for ADL and iADL tasks are given in Table A.1.

In the original paper by Katz et al. (1970), the ADL tasks were to be evaluated on a zero-one scale, i.e., a person could either be having a deficit or not, and no intermediate degrees of dependency could be selected. Yet, many assessment tools for long-term-care programmes in Europe now include an evaluation of ADL using a multivariate scale with several degrees of dependency for each task (e.g. complete dependency, partial dependency, light dependency).

The Lawton iADL taxonomy is binary as-well (Lawton & Brody, 1969), with patients being classifiable as "dependent" or "not dependent" with respect to each task, without intermediate values. The original scale includes a specific definition for "dependency" together with a list of *lighter* levels of dependency, which are anyway included into the "not dependent" category. As an example, consider the housekeeping dimension: there is one

A. Brugiavini et al., *Vulnerability and Long-term Care in Europe*,
https://doi.org/10.1007/978-3-319-68969-2

specific definition for "dependency", which is "not participating in any housekeeping task", alongside a list of lighter degrees of limitation (e.g. "performing only light daily tasks" or "needing help with all home tasks") which are anyway included in the "non-dependency" category.

Table A.1 ADL and iADL

ADL: activities of daily living	*iADL: instrumental Activities of daily living*
Bathing: dependency means "needing help with bathing in more than one part of the body", "getting in or out of the tub or shower", or "requiring total bathing".	**Ability to use the telephone**: dependency means "not using the telephone at all on own initiative". Lighter levels are: "dialing only a few well-known numbers" and "answering but not dialing".
Dressing: dependency means "needing help with self-dressing" or "needing to be completely dressed".	**Shopping**: Dependency means "shopping independently only for small purchases", "needing to be accompanied on any shopping trip" or "being completely unable to shop".
Use of WC: dependency means "needing help in transferring to the toilet, self-cleaning or using bedpan or commode".	**Food preparation**: dependency means "preparing adequate meals only if supplied with ingredients", "heating and serving prepared meals", "preparing meals but being unable to maintain adequate diet" or "needing to have meals prepared and served".
Transferring: dependency means "needing help in moving from bed to chair" or "requiring a complete physical transfer".	**Housekeeping:** dependency means "not participating in any housekeeping tasks". Lighter levels include "performing only light daily tasks while being unable to maintain acceptable level of cleanliness" and "needing help with all home maintenance tasks".
Continence: dependency means "being partially or totally incontinent of bowel or bladder"	**Doing laundry:** dependency means "being unable to do laundry". Lighter levels include "laundering only small items and rinsing stocks and stockings".
Nutrition: dependency means "needing partial or total help with feeding" or "requiring parenteral feeding".	**Mode of transportation**: dependency means "travelling only with taxi or automobile, with assistance of another" or "not travelling at all". Lighter levels include: "travelling independently with taxi-only" and "travelling on public transportation when accompanied by another".
	Responsibility for own medications: dependency means "being incapable of dispensing own mediation, except maybe for those already prepared in advanced and in separate dosages".
	Ability to handle finances: dependency means "being incapable of handling money". Lighter levels include "being able to manage day-to-day purchases while needing help with banking, major purchases etc".

Italian Regional Assessment Scales (Tables A.2, A.3, A.4, A.5, A.6, A.7, A.8, A.9, A.10, and A.11)

Table A.2 The BINA Scale for the Emilia-Romagna Region

Limitation	*Description*
Medications needed	10: Not needed 30: For ulcers 60: for catheters 100: For bedsores
Medical care needed	10: No (in good health) 30:Can receive scheduled care in hospital 70: Domiciliary care needed 100: Full-time care needed
Controlling bladder	10: Full control 30: Rare episodes 70: Frequent episodes 100: Fully incontinent
Behavioural issues	10: No 50: Mood issues 80: Cognitive issues 100: Cognitive and behavioural issues (aggressive/ disturbing behaviours)
Communication	10: Understands and talks 40: Difficulties in communication 70: Difficulties in understanding and communication 100: Unable to understand
Sensory impairment (sight and hearing)	10: None 20: Can use visual or hearing aids 80: Incurable impairment 100: Fully deaf and/or blind
Mobility	10: Autonomous 30: Able to move with aids 80: Needs help from others 100: Bedridden
Daily living activities (personal hygiene, dressing, eating)	10: Fully independent 20: Needs occasional help 70: Needs frequent help 100: Fully dependent
Social network	10: Can rely on family 30: Can partially rely on family, or receives informal care from outside the household 60: Informal care only available if summoned by local authorities 100: Can't rely on anyone

(*continued*)

Table A.2 (continued)

Limitation	*Description*
Housing quality and environment	10: Good housing quality, services available close by 20: In-house barriers impede access to services nearby 70: Barriers impede access to crucial in-house areas (kitchen, bathroom) 100: Crucial in-house facilities are lacking

Source: Azienda Unità Sanitaria Locale di Bologna, resolution n. 113 (27/06/2006)

Table A.3 Assessment-of-need for Friuli—Venezia Giulia's CAF and APA

Limitations	*Evaluation*	*Description*
Bathing	Yes/no	Needs help with bathing more than one part of the body, getting in or out of the tub or shower
Dressing	Yes/no	Needs help with dressing self or needs to be completely dressed
Use of WC	Yes/no	Needs help transferring to the toilet, cleaning self or uses bedpan or commode
Transferring	Yes/no	Needs help in moving from bed to chair or requires a complete transfer
Continence	Yes/no	Is partially or totally incontinent of bowel or bladder
Nutrition	Yes/no	Needs partial or total help with feeding or requires parenteral feeding
Cognitive impairment	Yes/no	Is affected by dementia or has substantial sensory deficits (score of 3 on the Clinical Dementia Rating scale)

Source: Regional Law 6/2006

Table A.4 Health assessment for Liguria's Assegno di Cura

Outcome	*Evaluation*
Unable to feed	Yes/no
Unable to dress	Yes/no
Unable to bath	Yes/no
Need help in moving inside/ outside dwelling	Yes/no
Cognitive, Behavioural issues	Yes/no

Source: Regional Resolution 219/2008

Table A.5 TRIAGE assessment scale in Lombardia

Outcome	*Level 1*	*Level 2*	*Level 3*	*Level 4*
1. Morbidity	Absent or mild (0)	Moderate (1)	High (2)	Very high (2)
2. Eating	Autonomous (0)	With supervision (0)	Severe dependency (1)	Enteral or parenteral nutrition (2)
3. Continence	Continent (0)	Urinary incontinence/ faecal continence (0)	Urinary and faecal incontinence (nappies can be used) (1)	Urinary and faecal incontinence (catheters needed) (1)
4. Mobility	Autonomous (0)	Minimal help needed (0)	Limited (1)	Bedridden (2)
5. Personal hygiene	Autonomous (0)	Minimal help needed (0)	Limited (1)	Entirely dependent (2)
6. Mental and behavioural issues	None (0)	Cooperative, with cognitive issues (0)	Uncooperative, with cognitive issues (1)	Uncooperative, with cognitive or behavioural issues (1)
7. Living arrangement	Living with partner/family/ assistant (0)	Living alone, not needing assistance (0)	Living alone or with someone, needing assistance/ network (1)	Living alone, lacks network/ assistance (2)
8. Care received	Adequate (0)	Partially adequate (1)	Inadequate (2)	No assistance is given (2)

Source: Resolution of Direttore Generale della DG Famiglia, Conciliazione, Integrazione e Solidarietà Sociale n. 6032/2012

Table A.6 ADL and iADL reverse scale for Lombardia

Outcome	*Evaluation*
Bathing	1: does not need help, or needs help in washing one part of the body 0: needs help in washing more than one body part
Dressing	1: does not need help for dressing, or needs help in putting on shoes only 0: needs help in dressing either the entire body or a part
Use of WC	1: uses the toilet without help 0: needs help in using the toilet, or cannot go to the toilet

(*continued*)

Table A.6 (continued)

Outcome	*Evaluation*
Transferring	1: gets in and out of bed without help 0: needs help in getting in and out of bed, or is bedridden
Continence	1: incontinent of bowel and bladder 0: has occasional incidents, or cannot control continence of bowel/bladder
Nutrition	1: eats without help, or needs help in cutting up the food 0: needs help for eating, or needs enteral/parenteral nutrition
Ability to use the telephone	1: able to use the phone, even to call only few numbers, even if only able to answer 0: unable to use the telephone
Shopping	1: takes care of all the groceries' purchases 0: only able to shop in small shops, or needs to be accompanied, or is totally unable to make purchases
Mode of transportation	1: goes out alone, uses own car or public transport, or taxi without help, or needs to be accompanied on public transport 0: can only use taxi with help, or cannot go out
Responsibility for self-medications	1: autonomous, can take care of dosages 0: can only manage pre-prepared medications, or is not able to take own medicines
Ability to handle finances	1: independent in dealing with bank operations, or just with everyday payments 0: unable to handle money or finances
Food preparation	1: autonomous in preparing food 0: eats pre-prepared food, or needs to be help with ingredients
Housekeeping	1: independent for doing light works, or needs some help 0: unable to do any task
Doing laundry	1: does all the laundry by herself, or just the underwear 0: laundry is entirely done by others

Source: application form issued by the Municipalities Consortium District n.5 (Ambito territoriale Distretto 5, Municipalities of Cassano d'Adda, Inzago, Liscate, Melzo, Pozzuolo Martesana, Settala, Truccazzano, Vignate), available at http://www.comune.melzo.mi.it/wp-content/uploads/2017/02/domanda-voucher-ANZIANI.pdf

Table A.7 The Health components of Piemonte's Cartella Geriatrica assessment scale

Dimensions	*Categories*		
Functional autonomy (Barthel Functional)	0–14	15–49	50–60
Score for Cartella Geriatrica	0	2	3
Mobility (Barthel Mobility)	0–14	15–29	30–40
Score for Cartella Geriatrica	0	2	3
iADL	10–14	5–9	0–4
Score for Cartella Geriatrica	0	1	2
SPMSQ (mental deterioration): number of mistakes	0–4	5–7	8–10
Score for Cartella Geriatrica	0	1	2
Behavioural issues	None	Mild	Severe
Score for Cartella Geriatrica	0	1	2

Source: Regional Resolution DGR 42-8390/2008

Table A.8 The Piemonte's Barthel scale (Functional and Mobility)

Limitation in	*Assessment values*
Functional	
Feeding	0/2/5/8/10
Bathing self	0/1/2/4/5
Personal toilet	0/1/2/4/5
Dressing	0/2/5/8/10
Controlling bowels	0/2/5/8/10
Controlling bladder	0/2/5/8/10
Using the toilet	0/2/5/8/10
Mobility	
Moving from chair to bed and return	0/3/8/12/15
Walking on level surface	0/3/8/12/15
Ascend and descend stairs	0/2/5/8/10

Table A.9 iADL reverse scale in Piemonte's Cartella Geriatrica

Outcome	*Level 1*	*Level 2*	*Level 3*	*Level 4*
Ability to use the telephone	(3) Autonomous in using the phone	(2) Only able to dial a few well-known numbers	(1) Only able to answer the phone	(0) Unable to use the telephone
Shopping	(3) Autonomous in shopping	(2) Only able to make small purchases	(1) Needs help of any kind of purchase	(0) Unable to go shopping
Mode of transportation	(4) Autonomous; (3) uses taxi but not public transport	(2) Uses public transport if accompanied	(1) Only able to use taxi and only if accompanied	(0) Cannot use any mode of transportation
Responsibility for self-medications	(2) able to assume any medicine	(1) Only able to use pre-prepared doses	–	(0) Unable to assume medicines or follow prescriptions
Ability to handle finances	(2) Able to handle finances	(1) only able to handle daily purchases	–	(0) Unable to handle money or finances

Table A.10 iADL reverse scale for Piemonte's Cartella Geriatrica

Outcome	*Evaluation*
Ability to use the telephone	3/2/1/0
Shopping	3/2/1/0
Mode of transportation	4/3/2/1/0
Responsibility for self medications	2/1/0
Ability to handle finances	2/1/0

Table A.11 The Sardegna's modified Barthel Scale and dataset correspondence

Limitation in	*Assessment values*
Functional	
Feeding	10/8/5/2/0
Bathing self	5/4/3/1/0
Personal toilet	5/4/3/1/0
Dressing	10/8/5/2/0
Controlling bowels	10/8/5/2/0
Controlling bladder	10/8/5/2/0
Using the toilet	10/8/5/2/0
Mobility	
Moving from chair to bed and return	15/12/8/3/0
Walking on level surface	15/8/5/2/0
Ascend and descend stairs	10/8/5/2/0

Source: Regional Resolution 33/12, 2015

Notes

1. Further details of ADL and iADL can be found in seminal works by Katz, Downs, Cash, and Grotz (1970) and Lawton and Brody (1969) as well as in Shelkey and Wallace (1998) (for ADL) and Graf (2009) (for iADL).
2. On the hierarchical structure of ADL and iADL see Wiener, Hanley, Clark, and Van Nostrand (1990), Kempen, Myers, and Powell (1995), Thomas, Rockwood, and McDowell (1998), LaPlante (2010). As LaPlante (2010) highlights, the paediatric development model implicit in the ADL scale implies that "as a child matures, the simplest activity, eating, is mastered first, then continence, transferring, toileting, dressing, and bathing, in order of increasing complexity. As a person ages, or experiences certain chronic illnesses, performance is lost in the reverse order, from bathing to eating".

References

Graf, C. (2009). The Lawton instrumental activities of daily living (IADL) scale. *The Gerontologist*, *9*(3), 179–186.

Katz, S., Downs, T. D., Cash, H. R., & Grotz, R. C. (1970). Progress in development of the index of ADL. *The Gerontologist*, *10*(1 Part 1), 20–30. https://doi.org/10.1093/geront/10.1_Part_1.20

Kempen, G. I. J. M., Myers, A. M., & Powell, L. E. (1995). Hierarchical structure in ADL and IADL: Analytical assumptions and applications for clinicians and researchers. *Journal of Clinical Epidemiology*, *48*(11), 1299–1305. https://doi.org/10.1016/0895-4356(95)00043-7

LaPlante, M. P. (2010). The classic measure of disability in activities of daily living is biased by age but an expanded IADL/ADL measure is not. *The Journals of Gerontology Series B: Psychological Sciences and Social Sciences*, *65*(6), 720–732. https://doi.org/10.1093/geronb/gbp129

Lawton, M. P., & Brody, E. M. (1969). Assessment of older people: Self-maintaining and instrumental activities of daily living. *The Gerontologist*, *9*(3), 179–186.

Shelkey, M., & Wallace, M. (1998). Katz index of independence in activities of daily living (ADL). *The Gerontologist*, *10*(1), 20–30.

Thomas, V. S., Rockwood, K., & McDowell, I. (1998). Multidimensionality in instrumental and basic activities of daily living. *Journal of clinical epidemiology*, *51*(4), 315–321.

Wiener, J. M., Hanley, R. J., Clark, R., & Van Nostrand, J. F. (1990). Measuring the activities of daily living: Comparisons across national surveys. *Journal of Gerontology*, *45*(6), S229–S237.

Index

A. Brugiavini et al., *Vulnerability and Long-term Care in Europe*,
https://doi.org/10.1007/978-3-319-68969-2

MIX
Papier aus verantwortungsvollen Quellen
Paper from responsible sources
FSC® C105338
FSC
www.fsc.org

Printed by Books on Demand, Germany